W9-CBM-185

student book volume 1

Cultural, Social and Technical

MATHEMATICS

Secondary Cycle Two, Year Three

Claude Boivin
Dominique Boivin
Antoine Ledoux
Étienne Meyer
François Pomerleau
Vincent Roy

LES ÉDITIONS CEC
A Quebecor Media Company

9001, boul. Louis-H.-La Fontaine, Anjou, Québec, Canada H1J 2C5
Telephone: 514 351-6010 • Fax: 514 351-3534

ORIGINAL VERSION

Publishing Manager
Véronique Lacroix

Production Manager
Danielle Latendresse

Coordination Manager
Rodolphe Courcy

Project Manager
Dany Cloutier
Diane Karneyeff

Proofreader
Viviane Deraspe

Graphic Design
Dessine-moi un mouton

Technical Illustrations
Stéphan Vallières

General Illustrations
Rémy Guenin

Geographical Maps
Les Studios Artifisme

Iconographic Research
Jean-François Beaudette

The authors and publisher wish to thank the following people for their collaboration in the evolution of this project.

Collaboration
Richard Cadieux, consultant expert, école secondaire Jean-Baptiste-Meilleur, CS des Affluents

Scientific Consultant
Matthieu Dufour, professor, UQAM

Consultation pédagogique
Johanne Robert, Teacher, École Secondaire Louis-Cyr, CS des Grandes-Seigneuries
Stéphane Rompré, Teacher, École Secondaire Léopold-Gravel, CS des Affluents
Mélanie Tremblay, Teacher, UQAR

ENGLISH VERSION
Translation of *Visions,* Culture, société et technique, manuel de l'élève, volume 1, 3e année du 2e cycle du secondaire by i-EDIT inc.

These programs are funded by Quebec's Ministère de l'Éducation, du Loisir et du Sport, through contributions from the Canada-Québec Agreement on Minority-Language Education and Second-Language Instruction.

Visions, Cultural, Social and Technical, *Student Book*, Volume 1, Secondary Cycle Two, Year Three
© 2010, Les Éditions CEC inc.
9001, boul. Louis-H.-La Fontaine
Anjou (Québec) H1J 2C5

Translation of *Visions,* Culture, société et technique, manuel de l'élève, volume 1, 3e année du 2e cycle du secondaire
ISBN 978-2-7617-2799-0
© 2009, Les Éditions CEC inc.

Legal Deposit: 2010
Bibliothèque et Archives nationales du Québec
Library and Archives Canada

ISBN 978-2-7617-2802-7

Printed in Canada
1   2   3   4   5   14   13   12   11   10

TABLE OF CONTENTS

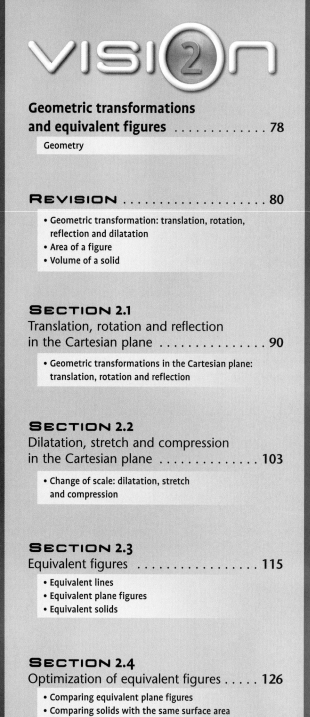

PRESENTATION OF STUDENT BOOK

This *Student Book* contains two chapters each called "Vision." Each "Vision" presents various learning and evaluation situations (LES), a "Revision," sections and special features "Chronicle of the past," "In the workplace," "Overview" and "Bank of problems." At the end of the *Student Book*, there is the "Learning and evaluation situations" section and the "Reference" section.

REVISION

The "Revision" section helps to reactivate prior knowledge and strategies that will be useful in each "Vision" chapter. This feature contains several activities designed to review prior learning, a "Knowledge summary" which provides a summary of the theoretical elements being reviewed and a "Knowledge in action" section consisting of reinforcement exercises on the concepts involved.

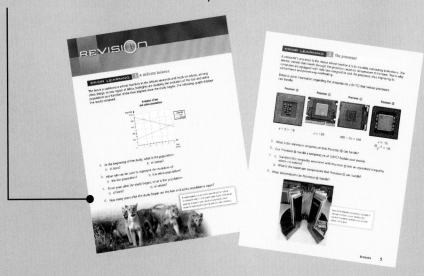

THE SECTIONS

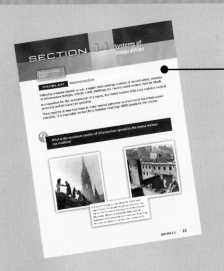

A "Vision" chapter is divided into sections, each starting with a problem and a few activities, followed by the "Technomath," "Knowledge" and "Practice" features. Each section is related to an LES that contributes to the development of subject-specific and cross-curricular competencies as well as to the integration of mathematical concepts that underscore the development of these competencies.

Problem

The first page of a section presents a problem that serves as a launching point and is made up of a single question. Solving the problem engages several competencies and various strategies while calling upon the mobilization of prior knowledge.

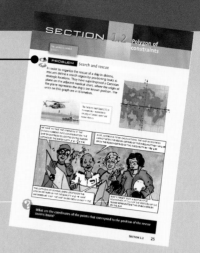

Activity

The activities contribute to the development of subject-specific and cross-curricular competencies, require the use of various strategies, mobilize knowledge and further the understanding of mathematical notions. These activities can take on several forms: questionnaires, material manipulation, simulations, historical texts, etc.

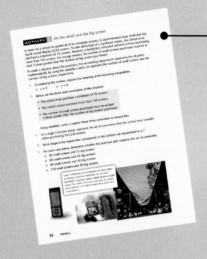

Technomath

The "Technomath" sections allows students to use technological tools such as a graphing calculator, dynamic geometry software or a spreadsheet program. In addition, the section shows how to use these tools and offers several questions in direct relation to the mathematical concepts associated with the content of the chapter.

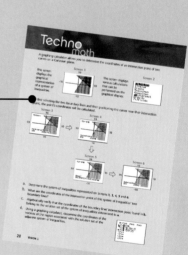

Knowledge

The "Knowledge" section presents a summary of the theoretical elements encountered in the section. Theoretical statements are supported with examples in order to foster students' understanding of the various concepts.

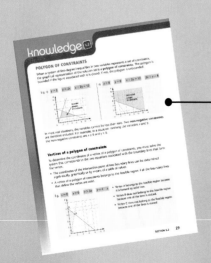

Practice

The "Practice" section presents a series of contextualized exercises and problems that foster the development of the competencies and the consolidation of what has been learned throughout the section.

Chronicle of the past

The "Chronicle of the past" feature recalls the history of mathematics and the lives of certain mathematicians who have contributed to the development of mathematical concepts that are directly related to the content of the "Vision" chapter being studied. This feature includes a series of questions that deepen students' understanding of the subject.

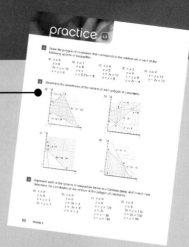

In the workplace

The "In the workplace" feature presents a profession or a trade that makes use of the mathematical notions studied in the related "Vision" chapter. This feature includes a series of questions that deepen students' understanding of the subject.

Overview

The "Overview" feature presents a series of exercises and contextualized problems that integrate and consolidate the competencies that have been developed and the mathematical notions studied.

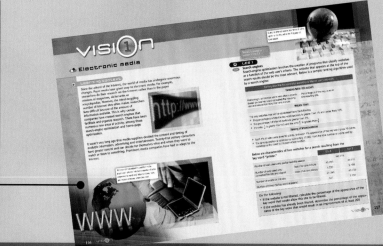

The "Knowledge in action," "Practice," "Overview" and "Bank of problems" features include the following:
- A number in a blue square refers to a Priority **1** and a number in an orange square a Priority **2**.
- When a problem refers to actual facts, a keyword written in red uppercase indicates the subject with which it is associated.

Bank of problems

This feature ends each "Vision" and presents problems, most of which are in context, each of which focuses on solving, reasoning or communication.

Learning and evaluation situations (LES)

The "Learning and evaluation situations" (LES) are grouped according to a common thematic thread; each focuses on a general field of instruction, a subject-specific competency and two cross-curricular competencies. The knowledge acquired through the sections helps to complete the tasks required in the LES.

REFERENCE

Located at the end of the *Student Book*, the "Reference" section contains several tools that support the student-learning process. It consists of two distinct parts.

The "Technology" part provides explanations pertaining to the functions of a graphing calculator, the use of a spreadsheet program as well as the use of dynamic geometry software.

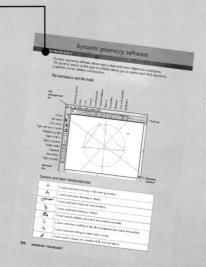

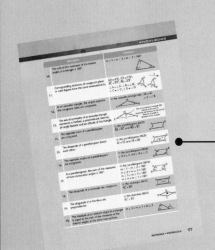

The "Knowledge" part presents notations and symbols used in the *Student Book*. Geometric principles are also listed. This part concludes with a glossary and an index.

ICONS

 Indicates that a worksheet is available in the *Teaching Guide.*

 Indicates that the activity can be performed in teams. Details on this topic are provided in the *Teaching Guide.*

 Indicates that some key features of subject-specific competency 1 are mobilized.

 Indicates that some key features of subject-specific competency 2 are mobilized.

 Indicates that some key features of subject-specific competency 3 are mobilized.

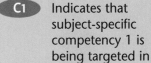 **C1** Indicates that subject-specific competency 1 is being targeted in the LES.

C2 Indicates that subject-specific competency 2 is being targeted in the LES.

C3 Indicates that subject-specific competency 3 is being targeted in the LES.

VISI1ON

Systems of equations and inequalities

Businesses in the 21st century require staff, machines and organizational structures that are more efficient. Whether the task is to make a product as cheaply and as quickly as possible or to generate maximum profits using a minimum of resources, the objective is optimal performance. How can a situation be optimized while taking all constraints into account? In "Vision 1," you will learn to use mathematics to define these constraints algebraically and to represent them graphically. You will then learn how to determine a situation's optimal solution according to the stated objective.

Arithmetic and algebra

- System of first-degree inequalities in two variables
- Polygon of constraints
- Optimizing function
- Optimizing a situation and making a decision using linear programming

Geometry   Graphs   Probability

PRIOR LEARNING 1 A delicate balance

The lion is a carnivorous animal that lives in the African savannah and feeds on zebras, among other things. In one region of Africa, biologists are studying the evolution of the lion and zebra populations as a function of the time elapsed since the study began. The following graph displays the results obtained.

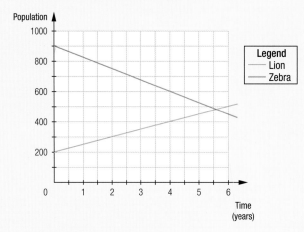

Evolution of lion and zebra populations

a. At the beginning of the study, what is the population:

   1) of lions?   2) of zebras?

b. What equation can be used to represent the evolution of:

   1) the lion population?   2) the zebra population?

c. Three years after the study began, what is the population:

   1) of lions?   2) of zebras?

d. How many years after the study began are the lion and zebra populations equal?

In some regions, groups of lions have refined their hunting techniques in order to catch specific types of prey. Some groups made up of roughly thirty lions have regularly been observed attacking adult elephants and even hippopotamuses.

A computer's processor is the device whose function it is to translate computing instructions. The electric current that travels through the processor causes its temperature to increase. That is why computers are equipped with little fans designed to cool the processor, thus improving its performance and preventing overheating.

Below is some information regarding the temperatures x (in °C) that various processors can handle.

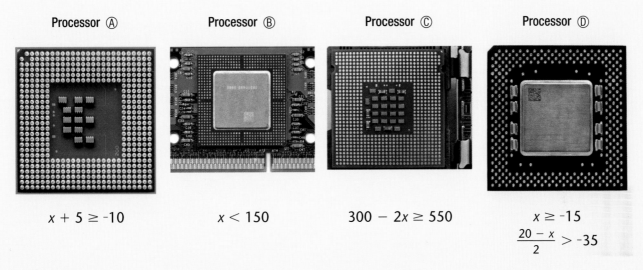

Processor Ⓐ

$x + 5 \geq -10$

Processor Ⓑ

$x < 150$

Processor Ⓒ

$300 - 2x \geq 550$

Processor Ⓓ

$x \geq -15$

$\dfrac{20 - x}{2} > -35$

a. What is the minimum temperature that Processor Ⓐ can handle?

b. Can Processor Ⓑ handle a temperature of 150°C? Explain your answer.

c. 1) Transform the inequality associated with Processor Ⓒ into an equivalent inequality where x is isolated.

2) What is the maximum temperature that Processor Ⓒ can handle?

d. What temperatures can Processor Ⓓ handle?

Some supercomputers produce large amounts of heat and must have a water-based cooling system to maintain temperatures that allow for optimal performance.

A chemical spill takes place in a neighbourhood. In order to determine the triangular area that must be evacuated, a Cartesian plane is superimposed onto a map of this neighbourhood. The units in the graph below are in decametres.

Map of neighbourhood

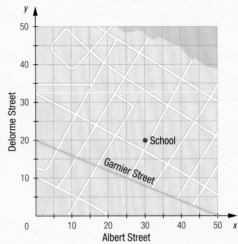

a. According to emergency services, the evacuation area is bound by Albert Street, Delorme Street and Garnier Street.

1) Determine the equation of the line associated with Garnier Street.

2) With respect to this street, determine the inequality that corresponds to the evacuation area.

3) Algebraically, show that the school is not within the evacuation area.

b. Following a change in the direction of the wind, emergency services decide that the evacuation area corresponds to the inequality $y \leq 40 - 0.5x$.

1) Graphically represent the evacuation area.

2) Is the school located in this area? Explain your answer.

c. Later still, strong winds force emergency services to re-evaluate the evacuation area. It now corresponds to the inequality $x + y < 50$.

1) Graphically represent the evacuation area.

2) Is the school located in this area? Explain your answer.

When land is polluted as the result of an accident or industrial activities, the set of processes undertaken to render the land suitable for residential or agricultural use is called decontamination.

SOLVING SYSTEMS OF EQUATIONS

A system of equations is a set of two or more equations. There are various strategies used for solving a system comprised of two first-degree equations in two variables. Solving a system involves determining which values simultaneously satisfy both equations in the system.

Graphical representation

In a graphical representation, the coordinates of the intersection point of two lines represent the solution of the system of equations associated with the two lines.

E.g. $y = -0.5x + 6$
$y = 0.75x + 1$

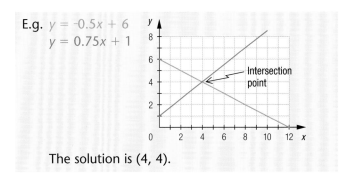

The solution is (4, 4).

Table of values

It is possible to obtain the solution of a system of equations by creating a table of values. You then search for a value for the independent variable for which the values of the dependent variable are identical.

E.g. $y = 2x + 1$
$y = -4x + 7$

x	y	y
-1	-1	11
0	1	7
1	3	3
2	5	-1
3	7	-5

The solution is (1, 3).

Algebraic methods

There are several algebraic methods used for solving a system of equations; these include the comparison method, the substitution method and the elimination method.

Comparison method	Substitution method	Elimination method
E.g. $y = 4x - 2$ $y = 3x + 4$	E.g. $3x + 2y = 5$ $y = -x - 4$	E.g. $-3x + 7y = 8$ $-4x + y = -6$
$4x - 2 = 3x + 4$ $x - 2 = 4$ $x = 6$	$3x + 2(-x - 4) = 5$ $3x - 2x - 8 = 5$ $x - 8 = 5$ $x = 13$	$\begin{matrix}-3x + 7y = 8\\-4x + y = -6\end{matrix} \Rightarrow \begin{matrix}-3x + 7y = 8\\-28x + 7y = -42\end{matrix}$ $\times 7$
$y = 4(6) - 2$ $y = 22$	$y = -(13) - 4$ $y = -17$	$\begin{matrix}-3x + 7y = 8\\- \ -28x + 7y = -42\end{matrix}$ $\begin{matrix}25x = 50\\x = 2\end{matrix}$ $25x \quad = 50$
The solution is (6, 22).	The solution is (13, -17).	$-3(2) + 7y = 8$ $y = 2$
		The solution is (2, 2).

INEQUALITY

An inequality is a mathematical statement that allows the comparison of two numerical expressions by means of an inequality symbol.

Inequality symbol	Meaning	Example
$<$	"is less than" or "is smaller than"	$8 < 8.1$
$>$	"is greater than" or "is bigger than"	$7 > 4.99$
$\leq$	"is less than or equal to" or "is smaller than or equal to"	$-10 \leq -5$
$\geq$	"is greater than or equal to" or "is bigger than or equal to"	$2^3 \geq 2 \times 3$

INEQUALITIES INVOLVING VARIABLES

An inequality involving variables is a mathematical statement with one or more variables and an inequality symbol.

E.g. 1) $a < 2$ 2) $6b > 17$ 3) $-8 \leq 2c + 1$ 4) $2d - 5 \geq e$

Transformation rules for inequalities

Transformation rules for inequalities allow you to obtain equivalent inequalities, meaning inequalities with the same solution set.

	Examples of equivalent inequalities
• Adding or subtracting the same number from both sides of an inequality preserves the direction of the inequality symbol.	$2a + 5 > 6$ $2a + 5 + 3 > 6 + 3$ $2a + 8 > 9$
	$5a + 6 < 16$ $5a + 6 - 4 < 16 - 4$ $5a + 2 < 12$
• Multiplying or dividing both sides of an inequality by the same strictly positive number preserves the direction of the inequality symbol.	$3a - 2 \geq -16$ $5 \times (3a - 2) \geq 5 \times -16$ $15a - 10 \geq -80$
	$4 - 14a \leq 3$ $(4 - 14a) \div 2 \leq 3 \div 2$ $2 - 7a \leq 1.5$
• Multiplying or dividing both sides of an inequality by the same strictly negative number reverses the direction of the inequality symbol.	$-3a > 20$ $-5 \times -3a < -5 \times 20$ $15a < -100$
	$-2a + 4 \leq 12$ $(-2a + 4) \div -2 \geq 12 \div -2$ $a - 2 \geq -6$

FIRST-DEGREE INEQUALITY IN TWO VARIABLES

To translate information into a first-degree inequality in two variables, proceed as follows.

1. Identify the variable or variables in the situation.	E.g. The mean mass of a man is 75 kg and that of a woman is 60 kg. If the maximum mass that an elevator can support is 1580 kg, how many men and women can it support at the same time? The variables are: • the number of men: x • the number of women: y
2. Determine which expressions are to be compared.	Expression representing: • the mass of the people in the elevator: $75x + 60y$ • the elevator's maximum load: 1580
3. Write the inequality with the appropriate inequality symbol. Once the inequality has been established, it can be verified by replacing the variable or variables with numerical values.	Inequality: $75x + 60y \leq 1580$ Validation: The elevator can, for example, support 3 men and 5 women. By substituting 3 for x and 5 for y, you get $75 \times 3 + 60 \times 5 \leq 1580$, which gives $525 \leq 1580$.

A solution to an inequality in two variables corresponds to an ordered pair that satisfies the inequality. The set of all ordered pairs that satisfy an inequality in two variables is called the solution set.

Half-plane

The solution set for a first-degree inequality in two variables can be graphically represented in a Cartesian plane.

- All points whose coordinates satisfy an inequality are located on the same side of the straight line that corresponds to the equation that corresponds to the inequality. The set of these points forms a **half-plane** that represents the inequality's solution set. Usually, this half-plane is coloured or shaded.

- A half-plane's **boundary line** is a **solid** line when the equation is part of the inequality ($\leq$ or $\geq$) and is a **dotted** line when the equation is excluded ($<$ or $>$).

E.g. 1) Representation of the solution set of the inequality $y \leq x + 3$.

2) Representation of the solution set of the inequality $y > -0.5x + 6$.

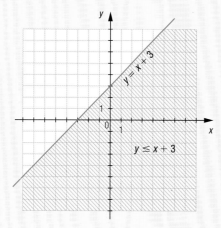

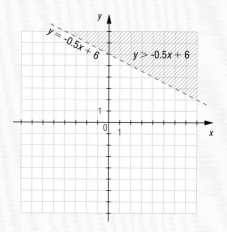

The solution set of a first-degree inequality in two variables can be graphically represented as follows.

1. Write the inequality in the form $y < ax + b$, $y > ax + b$, $y \leq ax + b$ or $y \geq ax + b$.	E.g. Graphically represent the solution set of the inequality $-x + 4y < -4$. $$-x + 4y < -4$$ $$4y < x - 4$$ $$y < 0.25x - 1$$
2. Draw the boundary line for the equation $y = ax + b$ with a solid line or a dotted line depending on whether the equation is part of the inequality or not.	The equation of the boundary line is $y = 0.25x - 1$. 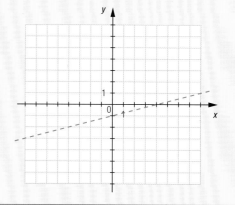
3. Colour or shade the half-plane below the line if the symbol is $<$ or $\leq$, or above the line if the symbol is $>$ or $\geq$.	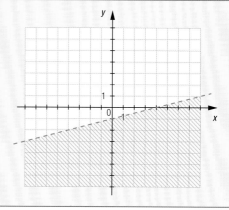

knowledge in action

1 Solve the systems of equations below.

a) $y = 3x + 2$
   $y = x - 7$

b) $3x + 6y = 180$
   $y = 4x + 8$

c) $x + 2y = 240$
   $x - 4y = 60$

d) $-6x + 2y = 18$
   $y = 3x - 16$

e) $3x + 5y = 30$
   $2x - 7y = 60$

f) $4y = 7x + 9$
   $2x - 5y = 100$

2 Solve each of the following inequalities.

a) $x + 9 \geq 3$

b) $2x - 7 < -2$

c) $-3x + 9 \leq 21$

d) $\frac{25 - 3x}{-4} > 13$

e) $-2x + 3 \geq x - 4$

f) $-\frac{x}{2} + 2 \leq x$

3 For each of the following inequalities, graphically represent the solution set in a Cartesian plane.

a) $x + y \geq 3$

b) $y < -2x + 10$

c) $2x + 5y \leq 40$

d) $y \geq 5$

e) $y > 2x$

f) $4x - 12y \geq 20$

g) $\frac{x}{2} + \frac{y}{3} \leq 2$

h) $x \leq 3$

4 Considering that the measure of angle B is at least 30° greater than half the measure of angle A, determine the possible measures of angle A for this triangle.

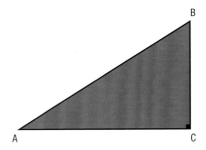

5 Translate each of the following situations into an inequality in one variable.

a) Three more than half of a certain number is not greater than 15.

b) Triple the opposite of a certain number is at least equal to 13 more than half that number.

c) If 10°C is subtracted from double the outside temperature, a temperature greater than 0°C is obtained.

6 For each of the situations below, do the following:

1) Identify the two unknowns and represent them using different variables.
2) Translate the situation into a system of equations.
3) Find the solution.

a) An elevator starts descending at a speed of 0.75 m/s from a height of 23 m. At the same time, a second elevator starts ascending at a speed of 0.5 m/s from a height of 2 m. At what height will the two elevators meet?

b) Two liquids are heated simultaneously in separate containers. The initial temperature of Liquid **A** is 40°C, and it then increases at a rate of 0.1°C/s. The initial temperature of Liquid **B** is 20°C, and it then increases at a rate of 0.3°C/s. When are the two liquids the same temperature?

c) Two moving objects are travelling around the same track in the same direction. At a certain point, the distance separating the two objects is 100 m. The speed of the first object is 8 m/s and that of the second is 10 m/s. How long will it take the second object to catch up with the first?

Formula 1 racing, which uses single-seater vehicles, is the most prestigious of all automobile races. There are, however, other racing categories such as NASCAR and IndyCar in the United States, as well as the 24-hour Le Mans, an endurance race.

d) The salary of Salesperson **A** is $200/week plus 20% of the amount of his or her weekly sales. The salary of Salesperson **B** is $120/week plus 40% of the amount of his or her weekly sales. For what sales amount do the two salespeople receive the same pay?

7 In each of the situations below, do the following:

1) Identify the two unknowns and represent them using different variables.
2) Translate the statement into a first-degree inequality in two variables.
3) Graphically represent the inequality's solution set.

a) In a group, there are at least 5 more boys than there are girls.

b) The speed of a cyclist is at least twice as great as that of a pedestrian.

c) The mass of a solvent is at least 10 times greater than that of a solute.

d) The number of people in a group comprised of men and women is exceeds 40.

e) If you subtract triple Julie's salary from double Jeanne's salary, the result does not exceed $15,000.

f) In a restaurant that has tables with 4 or 6 chairs, there are no more than 100 seats available.

8 Determine the inequality associated with each of the half-planes below.

a)

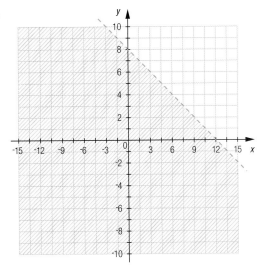

b)

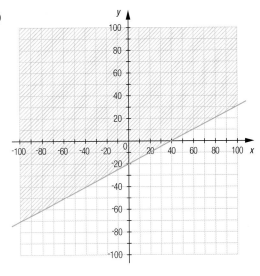

c)

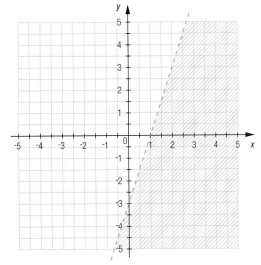

d)

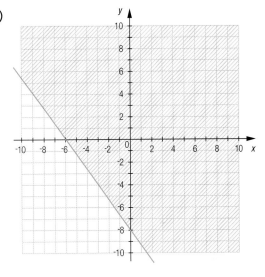

9 For each case, determine three ordered pairs that are part of the inequality's solution set.

a) $x + 3y \geq -5$

b) $y < -3x + 17$

c) $-2x + 7y \leq 9$

d) $x \leq -3$

e) $3y > 2x$

f) $-5x - 13y \geq 26$

g) $\dfrac{x}{4} + \dfrac{y}{7} \leq 42$

h) $y \geq 8.2$

10 The volume of the adjacent right trapezoidal-based prism is less than 90 cm³.

a) Express the inequality that describes this situation using the variables x and y.

b) In a Cartesian plane, represent the region where all ordered pairs (x, y) satisfy the condition stated above.

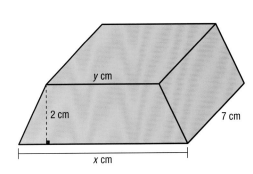

11 Match each inequality in the left column with the equivalent inequality in the right column.

Ⓐ $x - 2y > -3$		① $y < -0.5x + 1.5$	
Ⓑ $4x + 5y < -3y + 12$		② $y \geq 6x + 2$	
Ⓒ $-3x - \frac{y}{2} \leq 1$		③ $y > -1.5x - 0.5$	
Ⓓ $9x + 6y + 3 > 0$		④ $y > 1.5x + 0.5$	
Ⓔ $-\frac{3x}{2} + \frac{y}{4} \geq \frac{1}{2}$		⑤ $y < 0.5x + 1.5$	
Ⓕ $0 > 3 + 9x - 6y$		⑥ $y \geq -6x - 2$	

12 For each case, determine the inequality that is represented.

a)

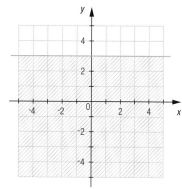

b)

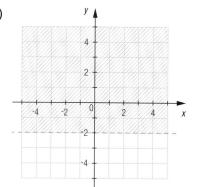

c)

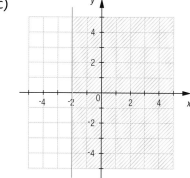

d)

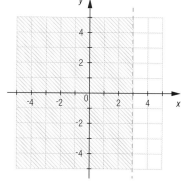

e)

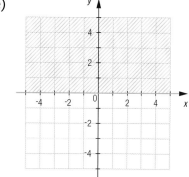

f)

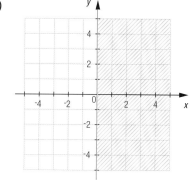

This section is related to LES 1.

PROBLEM   Reconstruction

Following a natural disaster or war, a region must undergo a period of reconstruction, whereby its infrastructure (bridges, schools, roads, buildings, etc.) and its social systems must be rebuilt.

In preparation for the reconstruction of a region, the United Nations (UN) must mobilize medical personnel and infrastructure specialists.

There must be at least four times as many medical personnel as one-third of the infrastructure specialists. It is impossible for the UN to mobilize more than 6000 people for this mission.

What is the maximum number of infrastructure specialists the United Nations can mobilize?

In France, the reconstruction that followed World War II lasted roughly 30 years. Paradoxically, this period is referred to as "The Glorious Thirty" because of the strong growth of both its population and economy. This was due, among other factors, to the full employment rate that stemmed from the need to rebuild everything. This period also marked the beginning of the consumer society.

The Ministry of Transport must equip itself with new vehicles in order to carry out work. Among these vehicles are excavators and rollers. Considering the work to be carried out, the following has been established:

• The number of rollers must be less than one-third the number of excavators.

• The total number of vehicles must not exceed 240.

This situation can be translated with the inequalities $x < \frac{1}{3}y$ and $x + y \leq 240$.

a. What do the variables x and y represent in each of the previous inequalities?

b. Below is the graphical representation of the solution sets for these inequalities. Match each graph with one of the two inequalities.

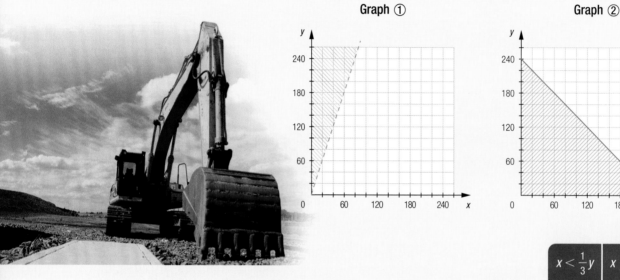

Graph ①

Graph ②

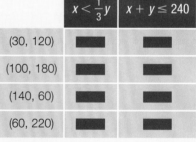

	$x < \frac{1}{3}y$	$x + y \leq 240$
(30, 120)		
(100, 180)		
(140, 60)		
(60, 220)		

c. For each of the inequalities in the adjacent table, indicate whether the suggested ordered pairs are solutions.

The two inequalities associated with this situation have been illustrated in the same Cartesian plane. The two boundary lines divide the plane into four regions.

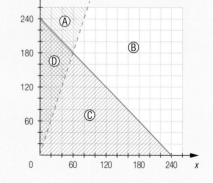

d. Which region or regions, shown in the adjacent Cartesian plane, contain points whose coordinates will satisfy:

1) the inequality $x < \frac{1}{3}y$?

2) the inequality $x + y \leq 240$?

3) both inequalities at once?

4) neither inequality?

e. Can the Ministry of Transport equip itself with 40 rollers and 120 excavators? Explain your answer.

Techno math

A graphing calculator allows you to represent the region associated with the solution set of one or more inequalities on a Cartesian plane.

These screens allow you to graphically represent the solution set of an inequality by first entering the equation of the boundary line, and then shading the region located on the appropriate side of the line.

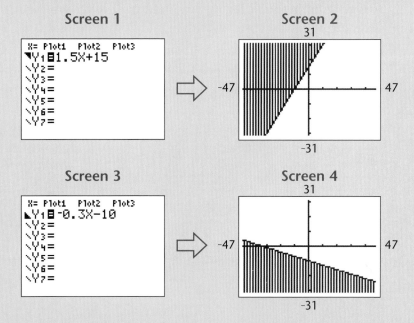

It is also possible to graphically represent the solution set of a system of inequalities. By moving the cursor on the graphical display, you can display an ordered pair that is inside or outside the solution set.

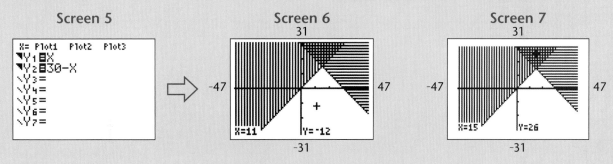

a. On Screens **1**, **3** and **5**, determine the meaning of:

  1) the ◥ symbol   2) the ◣ symbol

b. What is the inequality associated with:

  1) Screens **1** and **2**?   2) Screens **3** and **4**?

c. What is the system of inequalities associated with Screens **5**, **6** and **7**?

d. Algebraically demonstrate that the ordered pairs displayed:

  1) on Screen **6** do not belong to the solution set of the system of inequalities

  2) on Screen **7** belong to the solution set of the system of inequalities

e. Using a graphing calculator, display the solution set of each of the following systems of inequalities.

  1) $y \geq 2x - 5$ and $y \leq 0.5x + 12$.   2) $y \geq -x - 17.5$ and $y \geq x - 9$.

SYSTEM OF INEQUALITIES

A **system of inequalities** is comprised of at least two inequalities. The solution set of such a system:

• contains all ordered pairs that **simultaneously** satisfy all the system's inequalities

• graphically corresponds to the area of the plane that is common to the solution sets of all the inequalities that comprise the system

E.g. Representation of the solution set of this system of inequalities:

$$2x > 3y \qquad x + 6y \leq 12$$

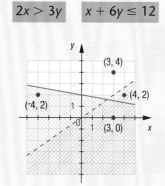

• Since the ordered pair (3, 4) does not satisfy either of the system's inequalities, it does not belong to the solution set.

• Since the ordered pair (-4, 2) only satisfies one of the system's two inequalities, it does not belong to the solution set.

• Since the ordered pair (4, 2) only satisfies one of the system's two inequalities, it does not belong to the solution set.

• Since the ordered pair (3, 0) satisfies all the system's inequalities, it belongs to the solution set.

Special systems of inequalities

When the boundary lines associated with a system of first-degree inequalities in two variables are parallel, some special situations arise.

E.g.

1) There is no solution.

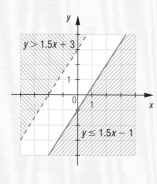

2) The solution set is comprised of ordered pairs satisfying the equation

$$y = \frac{7}{3}x - \frac{2}{3}.$$

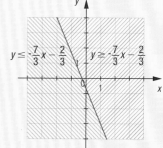

3) The solution set is comprised of ordered pairs satisfying the inequality $y > 0.4x + 0.6$.

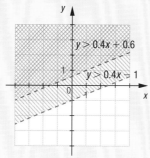

4) The solution set is comprised of ordered pairs associated with points located in the area between the two boundary lines.

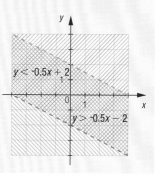

practice 1.1

1 For each case, graphically represent the solution set of the system of inequalities.

a) $y < -2x + 3$
   $y > x - 5$

b) $y \geq 0$
   $y < -5x + 20$

c) $y \geq \frac{2}{3}x + 3$
   $2x - 3y - 9 \geq 0$

d) $-2x + y \leq 0$
   $8x - 2y > -6$

2 a) The adjacent graph illustrates the two boundary lines of a system comprised of two inequalities. Identify the system of inequalities whose solution set corresponds to:

1) Region Ⓐ
2) Region Ⓑ
3) Region Ⓒ
4) Region Ⓓ

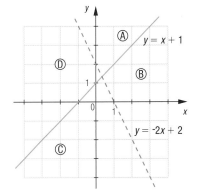

b) The adjacent graph illustrates the two boundary lines of a system comprised of two inequalities. Identify the system of inequalities whose solution set corresponds to:

1) Region Ⓐ
2) Region Ⓑ
3) Region Ⓒ
4) an empty set

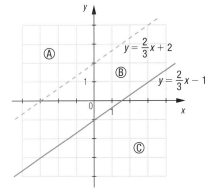

3 For each of the systems of inequalities below, identify, if possible, four ordered-pair solutions. If this is impossible, explain why.

a) $y < -3x + 2$
   $y > 2x - 3$

b) $y \geq 0.5x$
   $y > -5x + 20$

c) $y \geq \frac{4}{5}x + 3$
   $4x - 5y \geq 25$

d) $x - 2y \geq 0$
   $x - 2y \leq 0$

e) $y \geq x - 3$
   $y \leq 2x + 5$

f) $-3x + 2y > 12$
   $y \leq 1.5x + 6$

4 For each of the systems of inequalities below, determine whether points A(0, 0), B(2, 3), C(-4, 4), D(3, -2), E(-3, 2) and F(-5, -6) belong to the feasible region.

a) $y > 3x - 3$
$y \leq -x + 2$

b) $y < \frac{1}{2}x$
$y < 4x - 5$

c) $2x + 3y \geq 0$
$2x - 3y < 0$

d) $y \geq -3x + 3$
$y \leq -x + 5$

5 Identify the system of inequalities that is associated with each of the graphs below.

A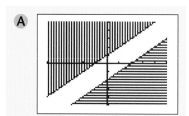

1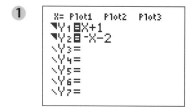

2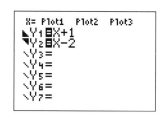

B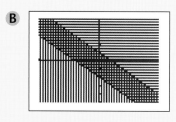

3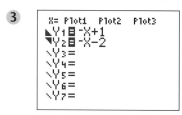

4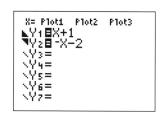

C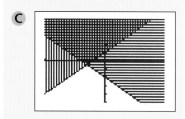

5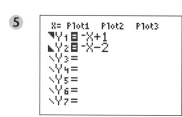

6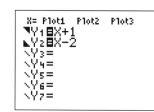

6 Among systems of inequalities below, which have a solution set that is:

a) empty?

b) represented by a half-plane?

c) represented by a straight line?

d) represented by a region bound by two non-coinciding parallel lines?

A $y > -x + 2$
    $y + x < 2$

B $5y > 2x - 3$
    $-y \leq -\frac{2}{5}x - 1$

C $y \geq \frac{3}{4}x$
    $4y \leq 3x$

D $-2x - 3y \leq 2$
    $-2x - 3y \geq 4$

E $-2x + 7y \leq 0$
    $-4x + 14y + 6 > 0$

7 a) Algebraically, represent each of the following situations using a system of inequalities in two variables.

Situation 1	Situation 2	Situation 3
The sum of two integers is greater than 6, and their difference is at most 18.	The sum of Leo and Lea's account balances is less than $0. In addition, double the opposite of Lea's account balance does not exceed triple Leo's bank balance.	The outside temperature in Quaqtaq is at most 3°C less than the outside temperature in Kuujjuaq. The sum of these temperatures is at most -35°C.

b) Graphically represent the solution set associated with each system.

c) Determine three ordered-pair solutions for each system.

8 For each case, identify the system of inequalities whose solution set is represented graphically.

a)

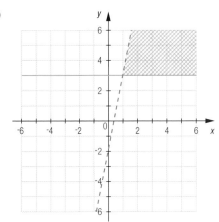

b)

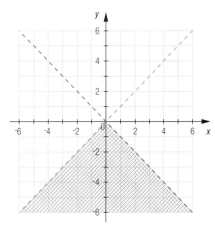

c)

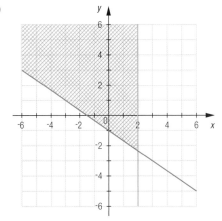

d)

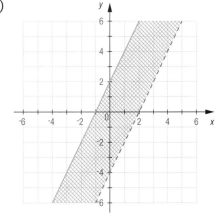

9 Among the systems of inequalities below, determine which have an empty set as a solution.

A $y \leq 3$
$y \leq 5$
$y > 11$

B $y \leq 0.5x$
$2y - x < -6$
$y > \frac{1}{2}x + 4$

C $y \geq -\frac{2}{5}x - 2$
$2x - 7y - 5 \geq 0$
$x < y$

D $y < 5x - 12$
$y \geq 4x - 3$
$y \geq -2x + 6$

10 For each case, determine, if possible, three ordered pairs that simultaneously satisfy:

a) the equation $y = {}^-3x + 15$ and the inequality $y \le 10x - 30$

b) the equation $y = x + 30$ and the inequalities $x < {}^-10$ and $y \ge {}^-3x - 7$

11 The equations of the boundary lines for the systems of inequalities represented below are $y = 2x + 5$ and $y = {}^-0.4x - 7$.

① 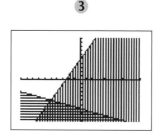   ②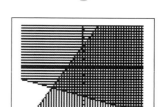

③   ④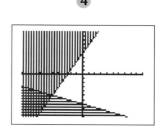

For each of the graphs, do the following:

a) Identify the associated system of inequalities.

b) Verify algebraically whether the ordered pair (-4, -4) belongs to the solution set.

12 A Cartesian plane is divided into four quadrants. Identify a system of inequalities whose graphical representation corresponds to:

a) the 1st quadrant

b) the 2nd quadrant

c) the 3rd quadrant

d) the 4th quadrant

13 Using the variables x and y, identify the system of inequalities with a solution set whose graphical representation corresponds to the following:

a) the set of points whose x-coordinates are strictly positive and whose y-coordinates are at least double the x-coordinates

b) the set of points whose y-coordinates are negative and whose x-coordinates are no more than one-third of the y-coordinates

c) the set of points whose y-coordinates are greater than the x-coordinates but no more than four times greater

14 The perimeter of a rectangular table is at most 480 cm, and its length is more than twice its width.

a) Represent this situation using a system of inequalities.

b) Determine the dimensions of three tables that satisfy the characteristics listed.

c) Among the rectangular tables illustrated below, determine which one satisfies the characteristics listed and has:

1) the greatest perimeter

2) the greatest area

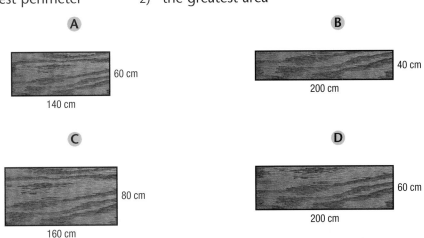

Ⓐ
60 cm
140 cm

Ⓑ
40 cm
200 cm

Ⓒ
80 cm
160 cm

Ⓓ
60 cm
200 cm

d) Determine the dimensions of a rectangular table that, in addition to satisfying the characteristics listed, has a greater area and a smaller perimeter than the table selected in question **c) 2)**.

15 **APGAR SCORE** At birth, babies undergo five tests to assess their health and receive 0, 1 or 2 points for each test. Afterwards, the baby is given a score of 0 to 10, with 10 representing a perfect bill of health.

If x represents the result on the pulse-rate test and y, the result on the breathing test, the following system of inequalities defines the conditions for the survival of a newborn.

$x > 0$
$y > 0$
$x \leq 2$
$y \leq 2$
$x + y \geq 2$
$x + y \leq 4$

The Apgar score was invented in 1952 by Dr. Virginia Apgar, the first woman doctor in history to be named head of a university department. In addition to the breathing and pulse-rate tests, the Apgar score also requires an examination of muscle tone, response to stimulation and skin colour.

a) In words, explain the meaning of each of the system's inequalities.

b) Graphically represent the solution set of this system of inequalities.

c) How many solutions, provided in the form ordered pairs, does this system allow?

16 Identify the system of inequalities whose solution set is illustrated below.

a)

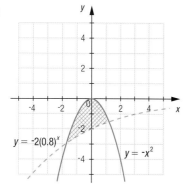

b)

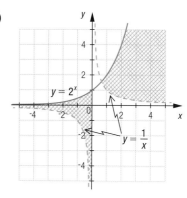

17 A system is comprised of the inequalities $y \geq \text{-}4x - 8$, $y \geq 2x - 6$ and $y \leq \text{-}x + 4$.

Each of the graphs below represents the solution set of one of this system's inequalities.

Graph ①

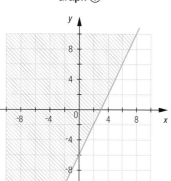

Graph ②

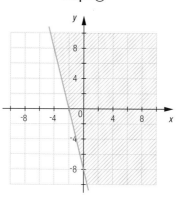

Graph ③

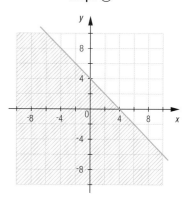

a) Match each graph above with the corresponding inequality.

b) Determine the coordinates of two points that:

1) satisfy the system of inequalities

2) do not satisfy the system of inequalities

18 The adjacent isosceles trapezoid has the following characteristics:

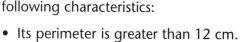

- Its perimeter is greater than 12 cm.

- Its area is less than or equal to 10 cm².

a) Can the bases of this trapezoid measure:

1) 3 cm and 5 cm?

2) 1 cm and 4 cm?

3) 4 cm and 7 cm?

4) 1 cm and 3 cm?

b) Using variables B and b, create a system of inequalities whose solution set corresponds to the possible dimensions of the trapezoid's bases.

c) Graphically represent the solution set of the system of inequalities associated with this situation.

Polygon of constraints

This section is related to LES 1.

PROBLEM Search and rescue

In order to organize the rescue of a ship in distress, rescuers define a search region by positioning boats at strategic locations. They have superimposed a Cartesian plane on the adjacent nautical chart, where the origin of the plane represents the ship's last known position. The units on this graph are in kilometres.

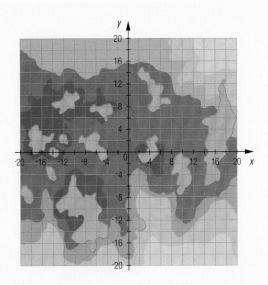

The Canadian Coast Guard (CCG) is the organization responsible for carrying out Canada's search and rescue missions.

WE HAVE TO TAKE THE STRENGTH OF THE OCEAN'S CURRENT INTO CONSIDERATION. THE SHIP IN DISTRESS IS LOCATED IN THE REGION DEFINED BY THE INEQUALITY $y \leq -\frac{6}{5}x + 12$.

ALSO, ACCORDING TO MY CALCULATIONS, THE SHIP IN DISTRESS CANNOT BE IN THE REGION DEFINED BY THE INEQUALITY $5y - 2x \geq 30$ OR IN THE REGION DEFINED BY THE INEQUALITY $6x - 10y \geq 60$.

THE CAPTAINS OF SEVERAL SHIPS LOCATED IN THE REGION DEFINED BY THE INEQUALITY $x \leq -4$ HAVE INFORMED ME THAT THE SHIP IN DISTRESS IS NOT THERE.

DON'T FORGET THAT A BOAT MUST BE POSITIONED AT EACH OF THE VERTICES OF THE FIGURE REPRESENTING THE SEARCH REGION ON THE MAP.

What are the coordinates of the points that correspond to the position of the rescue team's boats?

ACTIVITY 1 On the small and the big screen

In order for a school to update all of its computer screens, its administration buys small and big liquid crystal display (LCD) screens. To take advantage of a significant rebate, the school must purchase a minimum of 75 screens. However, a budgetary constraint prevents it from purchasing more than 150 screens. For storage reasons, the number of small screens purchased must be at least 3 times greater than the number of big screens purchased.

To make a decision about the purchase, the accounting department represents the situation mathematically by using the variables x and y to represent the number of small screens and the number of big screens, respectively.

a. Considering the context, explain the meaning of the following inequalities:

1) $x \geq 0$ 2) $y \geq 0$

b. Below are the three main constraints of this situation:

- The school must purchase a minimum of 75 screens.

- The school cannot purchase more than 150 screens.

- The number of small screens purchased must be at least 3 times greater than the number of big screens purchased.

Using variables x and y, express these three constraints as inequalities.

c. In a single Cartesian plane, represent the set of constraints that the school must consider when purchasing the LCD screens.

d. What shape is the region that corresponds to the solution set represented in **c.**?

e. For each case below, determine whether the purchase plan respects the set of constraints.
1)   30 small screens and 12 big screens
2)   60 small screens and 15 big screens
3)   90 small screens and 50 big screens
4)   110 small screens and 30 big screens

Liquid crystal display (LCD) revolutionized the visual industry by allowing screens to be miniaturized. They are found particularly in computers, cameras, cellular phones and digital players. The smallest LCD screen in the world has a surface area of less then 1 cm² while the largest has a surface area of over 6000 m².

ACTIVITY 2 A company's employees

Below are the constraints associated with the distribution of employees at two companies:

Company A

- The number of women is at least equal to three-quarters the number of men.

- The ratio of $\dfrac{\text{number of women}}{\text{number of men}}$ does not exceed $\dfrac{5}{2}$.

- The number of employees is less than or equal to 154.

Company B

- The number of employees is at least 154.

- The number of part-time employees is greater than three-quarters the number of full-time employees.

- The ratio of $\dfrac{\text{number of part-time employees}}{\text{number of full-time employees}}$ does not exceed $\dfrac{5}{2}$.

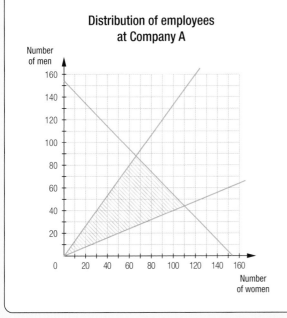

Distribution of employees at Company A

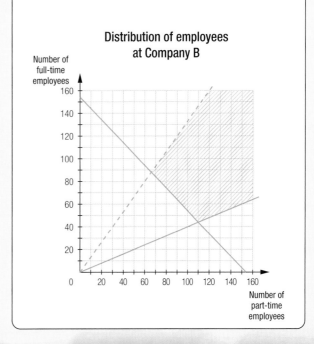

Distribution of employees at Company B

a. Determine the system of inequalities associated with:

   1) Company **A**   2) Company **B**

b. Describe the similarities and differences between the graphical representations associated with each of the companies.

c. 1) For each graph, algebraically determine the coordinates of the intersection point of the boundary lines that define the region representing the solution.

    2) For each of these points, indicate whether the coordinates belong to the solution set or not. Explain your answer.

Techno math

A graphing calculator allows you to determine the coordinates of an intersection point of two curves on a Cartesian plane.

Screen 1

This screen displays the graphical representation of a system of inequalities.

Screen 2

This screen displays various calculations that can be performed on the graphical display.

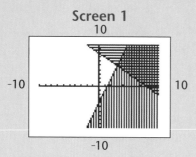

By first selecting the two boundary lines and then positioning the cursor near their intersection point, the point's coordinates will be calculated.

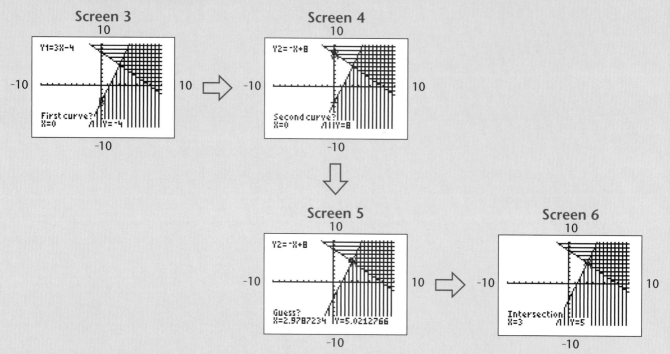

a. Determine the system of inequalities represented on Screens **1**, **3**, **4**, **5** and **6**.

b. What are the coordinates of the intersection point of this system of inequalities' two boundary lines?

c. Algebraically, verify that the coordinates of the boundary lines' intersection point found in **b.** belong to the solution set of the system of inequalities determined in **a.**

d. Using a graphing calculator, determine the coordinates of the vertices of the region associated with the solution set of the adjacent system of inequalities.

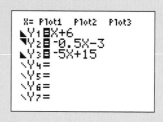

POLYGON OF CONSTRAINTS

When a system of first-degree inequalities in two variables represents a set of constraints, the graphical representation of the solution set is a **polygon of constraints**. The polygon is bounded if the figure associated with it is closed. If not, the polygon is unbounded.

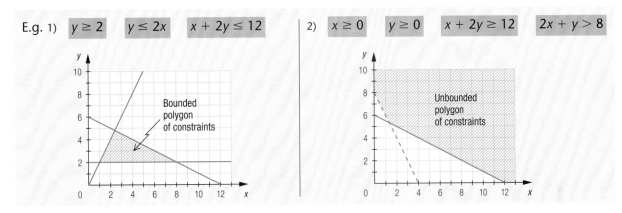

E.g. 1) $y \geq 2$ $y \leq 2x$ $x + 2y \leq 12$ 2) $x \geq 0$ $y \geq 0$ $x + 2y \geq 12$ $2x + y > 8$

In most real situations, the variables cannot be less than zero. Two **non-negative constraints** are therefore included. For example, in a situation involving the variables x and y, the non-negative constraints are $x \geq 0$ and $y \geq 0$.

Vertices of a polygon of constraints

To determine the coordinates of a vertex of a polygon of constraints, you must solve the system that corresponds to the two equations associated with the boundary lines that form the vertex.

- The coordinates of the intersection point of two boundary lines can be determined algebraically, graphically or by means of a table of values.

- A vertex of a polygon of constraints belongs to the feasible region if all the boundary lines that define the vertex are solid.

E.g. $x \geq 0$ $y > 3x$ $y \leq 4 - x$

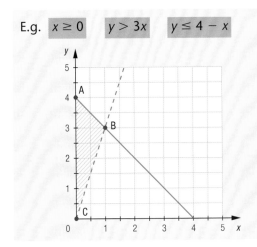

- Vertex A belongs to the feasible region because it is formed by solid lines.

- Vertex B does not belong to the feasible region because one of the lines is dotted.

- Vertex C does not belong to the feasible region because one of the lines is dotted.

1 Draw the polygon of constraints that corresponds to the solution set of each of the following systems of inequalities.

a) $x \geq 0$
$y \geq 0$
$2x + y \leq 10$
$x + y \leq 6$

b) $x \geq 1$
$x \leq 8$
$y \geq x$
$y \leq 0.25x + 8$

c) $x \geq 0$
$y \geq 0$
$x + 3y \geq 12$
$x + y \geq 8$

d) $x \geq 2$
$y \geq 0$
$x + y \leq 9$
$y \geq 2x - 8$

e) $x \geq 0$
$x + y \leq 12$
$x + 2y \geq 12$

2 Determine the coordinates of the vertices of each polygon of constraints.

a)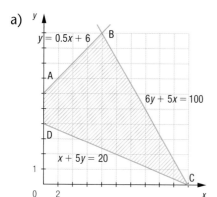

b)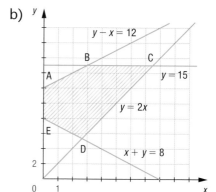

c)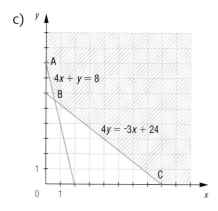

d)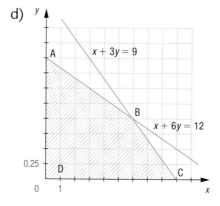

3 Represent each of the systems of inequalities below in a Cartesian plane, and in each case, determine the coordinates of the vertices of the polygon of constraints.

a) $x \geq 0$
$y \geq 0$
$x + y \geq 3$
$2x + y \leq 7$

b) $x \geq 0$
$y \geq 0$
$y \leq 3x + 3$
$y \leq -3x + 9$
$y \geq -x + 3$

c) $x \geq 0$
$y \geq 0$
$x + y \geq 120$
$y \leq 2x$
$y \geq x - 30$
$x + y \leq 180$

d) $x \geq 0$
$y \geq 0$
$3x + y \geq 135$
$x + 5y \geq 150$
$x + y \geq 90$

4 Below are systems of inequalities that represent constraints:

1) $x \geq 2$
   $y \geq 1$
   $-x + 2y \geq -2$
   $x + y \leq 8$

2) $x \geq 0$
   $y \geq 0$
   $y \geq -2x + 9$
   $y \geq -0.2x + 3$
   $y \geq -x + 7$

3) $x \geq 0$
   $y \geq 0$
   $3x + 2y \geq 120$
   $y \geq 3x - 20$
   $y \leq 2x + 30$
   $x + 0.5y \leq 80$

4) $x \geq 0$
   $y \geq 0$
   $3x - y \leq 150$
   $x + 5y \geq 125$
   $2x + y \geq 85$

For each of these systems, do the following:

a) Determine whether the graphical representation corresponds to a bounded or unbounded polygon of constraints.

b) Determine the coordinates of three points that belong to the polygon of constraints.

5 Below are two systems of inequalities that represent constraints:

1) $x \geq 0$
   $y \geq 0$
   $x + y \geq 10$
   $y < 2x + 4$
   $y > 0.5x - 2$

2) $y \geq 0.25x - 30$
   $4y + 3x + 160 > 0$
   $y - x < 45$
   $y \leq -2x + 10$

For each of these systems, do the following:

a) Determine the coordinates of the vertices of the polygon of constraints.

b) Indicate, for each vertex of the polygon of constraints, whether it belongs to the feasible region or not.

6 Refer to the adjacent graph and identify the system of inequalities whose solution set can be represented by polygon of constraints:

a) Ⓐ

b) Ⓑ

c) Ⓒ

d) Ⓓ

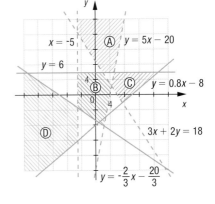

7 A kennel for dogs and cats cannot accommodate more than 75 animals at any given time. In addition, the number of cats cannot exceed more than two-thirds of the total number of animals.

a) Represent this situation using a polygon of constraints.

b) While respecting the constraints provided above, can this kennel accommodate:

1) 25 dogs and 50 cats?

2) 50 dogs and 25 cats?

3) 10 dogs and 40 cats?

4) 22 dogs and 51 cats?

c) Modify one of the constraints in this situation so that the kennel can accommodate 30 dogs and 65 cats.

8 Determine the system of inequalities associated with each polygon of constraints below.

a)

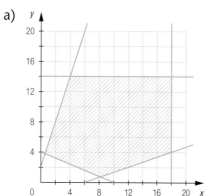

b)

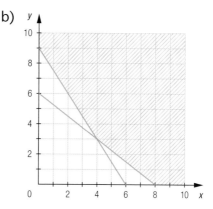

c)

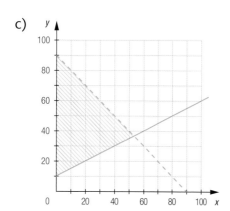

d)

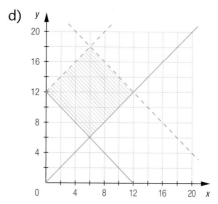

9 For each of the situations below, do the following:

1) Define the two variables.

2) Identify a system of inequalities that represents the constraints.

3) Graphically represent the polygon of constraints.

4) Determine the coordinates of the vertices of the polygon of constraints.

5) Provide five ordered pairs that satisfy the set of constraints.

a) Coniferous and deciduous trees must be planted to reforest an area. The number of deciduous trees must be more than double but less than quadruple the number of coniferous trees. In addition, the total number of trees to be planted must be greater than 800 without exceeding 1200.

b) The length of a rectangular enclosure must be at least 20 m more than double the width. The width must be at least 45 m. The perimeter of the enclosure cannot exceed 950 m.

c) Wood and metal posts must be used to support a new 50-km power line. There must be at least 20 posts for each kilometre. The number of metal posts must represent at least 20% and at most 45% of the total number of posts used to build the line.

d) The ratio of string instruments to wind instruments must be at least 3:2 for a symphony to be well-interpreted. In addition, the total number of instruments must be greater than 25. However, the orchestra cannot get more than 40.

10 During the development of a new residential area, space was created for a maximum of 12 new buildings comprised of single-family homes and condominiums. The number of buildings in each category cannot be zero, and the number of single-family homes must be at least double the number of condominiums.

a) Which of the two graphs below better represents this situation? Explain your answer.

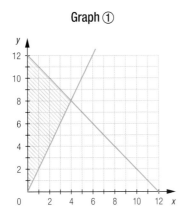

Graph ①

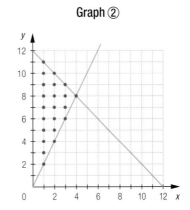

Graph ②

b) In this situation, is it true that the constraint $x > 0$ is equivalent to the constraint $x \geq 1$? Explain your answer.

11 A new clothing store must have fitting rooms installed. Below are the constraints associated with this situation:

① The total number of rooms must be greater than 10.

② The total number of rooms must not exceed 15.

③ There must be at least 5 rooms for women.

④ There must be at least 3 rooms for men.

⑤ The number of rooms for women must be greater than or equal to the number of rooms for men.

The polygon of constraints below represents this situation.

a) Match each constraint with one of the boundary lines.

b) One of this situation's constraints does not affect the number of fitting rooms installed. Which one? Explain your answer.

c) The store's manager claims that there are exactly 24 solutions that respect the set of constraints associated with this situation.

1) Explain why she is wrong.

2) Determine the exact number of possible solutions.

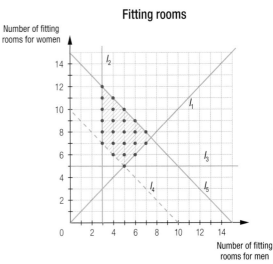

Fitting rooms

Number of fitting rooms for women

Number of fitting rooms for men

12 A company manufactures treaded tires and smooth tires for bicycles. It must use a truck to ship a minimum of 1500 tires, with at least 900 treaded tires and at least 400 smooth tires. To do this, the company packs the tires in two types of boxes whose contents are described in the table below.

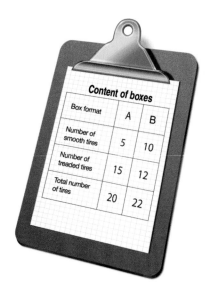

Content of boxes

Box format	A	B
Number of smooth tires	5	10
Number of treaded tires	15	12
Total number of tires	20	22

The biggest tire in the world measures over 4 m in diameter and is 1.57 m wide. This tire has a mass that exceeds 5 tons and each one costs approximately $50,000.

A truck cannot transport more than 120 boxes. If *x* represents the number of Format-**A** boxes and *y*, the number of Format-**B** boxes, do the following:

a) Draw the polygon of constraints associated with this situation.

b) Determine the coordinates of the vertices of this polygon of constraints.

13 A company wishes to acquire hard drives to be able to copy and save all its data. It must choose a certain number of drives from the two models described below.

Hard drive characteristics

Model	A	B
Price ($)	100	200
Capacity (GB)	200	500

Considering that the maximum budget is $8,000 and that the company must save over 25 000 GB of data, do the following:

a) Graphically represent the set of constraints associated with this situation.

b) Explain whether the characteristics of the models allow the company to respect the constraints.

A computer's hard drive is made up of many ridged discs that revolve an axis in a counter-clockwise manner. Information is saved in the form of a 0 or a 1 (called bytes). These discs are composed of fine, micron-thin, magnetic layers that are covered with a protective film.

14 **PHYSICAL TRAINING** During physical exertion, the Astrand formula allows for the determination of the maximum heart rate that the body can reach without danger, based on the age of the individual involved. The formula is as follows:

Maximum heart rate = 220 – age

This rate can vary up or down by 10 beats/min depending on the individual's initial fitness level.

During a training session, a specific heart rate can be targeted in order to obtain a certain result. The table below provides information on this topic, and the graph illustrates this situation for all individuals of a given age.

Physical training

Heart rate attained (% of maximum heart rate)	Targeted effect
[50, 60[	Maintaining current physical condition
[60, 65[	Mass reduction
[65, 85[	Improvement in cardiovascular capacities
[85, 110[	Intense training

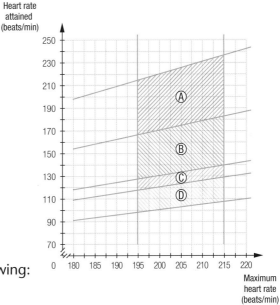

Heart rate attained during a training session

a) What is the age of the individuals represented in the adjacent graph?

b) For individuals of this age, do the following:

   1) Match each of the Zones Ⓐ, Ⓑ, Ⓒ and Ⓓ with the targeted effect.

   2) Provide the system of inequalities associated with the zone targeting mass reduction.

c) An individual's maximum heart rate, of this age, is 200 beats/min. This person wants to stay in the zone that targets mass reduction. What heart rates will allow this person to achieve this goal?

15 Describe a realistic situation whose solution set corresponds to the adjacent polygon of constraints.

This section is related to LES 1.

PROBLEM Transporting troops

The army has two types of land vehicles that are used to transport soldiers. Below are a few of these vehicles' characteristics:

Type of vehicle	Armoured car	Truck
Number of passengers	14	9
Mean speed (km/h)	66	100
Suspension	Torsion bar	Springs
Length (m)	5.31	6.32
Width (m)	2.69	2.55
Height (m)	1.86	2.08
Fuel efficiency (L/100 km)	17	10

During an exercise, as many soldiers as possible must be transported over a distance of 350 km while using at most 10 vehicles. Only 450 L of fuel are available, and the number of armoured vehicles must represent at least one-third and at most three-quarters of the total number of vehicles used. Below are four action plans:

TO BE EFFICIENT, WE SHOULD USE 5 VEHICLES OF EACH TYPE.

LET'S USE 3 ARMOURED CARS AND 6 TRUCKS INSTEAD.

THE MOST APPROPRIATE THING TO DO IS TO USE 6 ARMOURED CARS AND 2 TRUCKS.

WE SHOULD OBVIOUSLY TAKE 4 ARMOURED CARS AND 5 TRUCKS.

Identify a more efficient action plan than the ones suggested.

Operations research, a mathematical discipline that consists of finding the most effective solutions to a given problem, progressed enormously during World War II when the army called upon scientists to solve problems related to military logistics. In fact, the term "operations" was derived from its use in the military.

Making a good impression

A newspaper company needs to purchase new printers in order to print its daily edition. The newspaper's administration decides to order two types of printers.

Thermal printer: prints 75 pages/min

Laser printer: prints 100 pages/min

The total printing rate for all printers must be greater than 700 pages/min. The number of thermal printers must represent at least one-fifth and at most three-quarters of the total number of printers. Lastly, the total number of printers cannot exceed 13. A thermal printer costs $150,000 and a laser printer costs $250,000.

The variable x represents the number of thermal printers and the variable y, the number of laser printers.

a. 1) What equation allows you to calculate the cost C generated by the purchase of new printers?

2) Does this equation consider a constraint in this situation? Explain your answer.

b. Represent the set of constraints using a system of inequalities.

The polygon of constraints associated with this situation has been represented in the Cartesian plane below, and a few points have been identified.

Thermal printers and laser printers

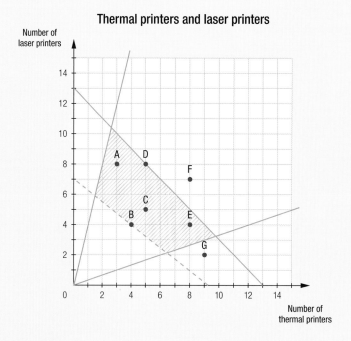

Number of laser printers

Number of thermal printers

c. Complete the table below.

Calculation of purchase cost

Point	Cost ($)
A(3, 8)	150,000 × 3 + 250,000 × 8 = 2,450,000
B(4, 4)	
C(5, 5)	
D(5, 8)	
E(8, 4)	
F(8, 7)	
G(9, 2)	

d. Considering that the company's objective is to minimize the cost of buying printers, refer to the ordered pairs provided in the table above and answer the following:

1) Which ordered pair or pairs should not be considered? Explain your answer.

2) Which ordered pair or pairs provide the least advantageous solution? Explain your answer.

3) Which ordered pair or pairs provide the most advantageous solution? Explain your answer.

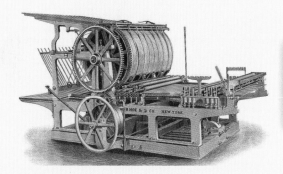

A newspaper press is also called a rotary press. Its inventor, William Bullock (1813-1867), died following an accident in which his leg was caught between two rollers in a newspaper press.

Techno math

A graphing calculator allows you to visualize ordered-pair solutions for a system of inequalities and perform calculations involving those ordered pairs.

Screen 1

Screen 2

This screen displays the equations of a system of inequalities' boundary lines as well as their graphical representation.

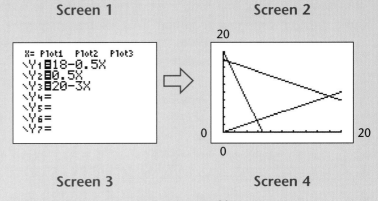

Screen 3

Screen 4

This screen displays some ordered-pair solutions for the system of inequalities.

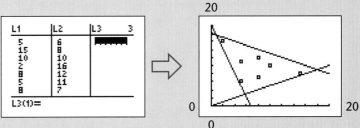

Screen 5

Screen 6

You can perform calculations involving these ordered pairs and store the results in a list.

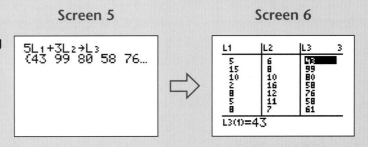

a. Identify the system of inequalities associated with the region in which the points are located in Screen **4**.

b. The values entered in lists L_1 and L_2 in Screens **3** and **6** correspond to ordered pairs (x, y). What algebraic expression allows you to obtain the values displayed in list L_3 in Screens **5** and **6**?

c. Among the ordered pairs in Screen **6**, which generates:
  1) the maximum value?   2) the minimum value?

d. 1) Using a graphing calculator, display the boundary lines associated with the adjacent system of inequalities and the points with coordinates (2, 4), (18, 7), (7, 10), (6, 5), (5, 12), (12, 8) and (4, 7).

$$y \geq 0.4x + 2$$
$$y \leq 4x$$
$$y \leq -0.8x + 18$$

  2) Among these seven ordered pairs, which generates:
    i) the maximum value of the expression $8x - 3y$?
    ii) the minimum value of the expression $4x - 0.5y$?

THE OPTIMIZING FUNCTION

In some situations involving a set of constraints, the target objective constitutes the search for the most advantegeous solution. This solution may correspond to the highest value, called the **maximum** or the lowest value, called the **minimum**. This optimal value is obtained using the rule of a function known as the **optimizing function**.

E.g. A company that makes windows in two different formats is looking to maximize its profits. Each week, it must make at least 150 windows, and the number of windows in Format **A** must not be more than double the number of windows in Format **B**. Each window in Format **A** generates a profit of $85, and each window in Format **B** generates a profit of $150.

Note the following about this situation:

- The company's objective is to maximize its profits.

- If x represents the number of windows in Format **A** and y, the number of windows in Format **B**, the rule of the optimizing function that allows you to calculate the weekly profit P (in $) is $P = 85x + 150y$.

ADVANTAGEOUS SOLUTIONS

An optimizing function whose rule is written in the form $z = ax + by + c$ allows you to compare ordered pairs (x, y) and to determine which among those ordered pairs constitutes the most advantageous solution, given the target objective.

E.g. Below is a polygon of constraints and the coordinates of various points. The rule of the optimizing function is $z = 4x + 2y$.

Point	$z = 4x + 2y$
A(1, 3)	$z = 4 \times 1 + 2 \times 3 = 10$
B(2, 2)	$z = 4 \times 2 + 2 \times 2 = 12$
C(2.5, 3.5)	$z = 4 \times 2.5 + 2 \times 3.5 = 17$
D(4, 2)	$z = 4 \times 4 + 2 \times 2 = 20$
E(4, 3)	$z = 4 \times 4 + 2 \times 3 = 22$

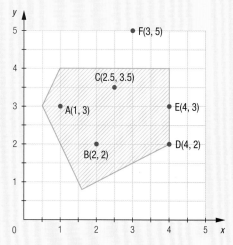

Among these points, note the following:

- Point F(3, 5) does not belong to the polygon of constraints. It can therefore not be considered.

- If the target objective is to maximize the function, the coordinates of point E(4, 3) represent the most advantageous solution.

- If the target objective is to minimize the function, the coordinates of point A(1, 3) represent the most advantageous solution.

practice 1.3

1 For each case, determine which among the suggested ordered pairs generates:

1) the maximum of the optimizing function   2) the minimum of the optimizing function

a)

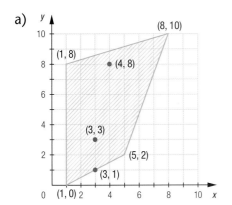

Ordered pair	$z = 4x - 2y$
(1, 0)	
(1, 8)	
(3, 1)	
(3, 3)	
(4, 8)	
(5, 2)	
(8, 10)	

b)

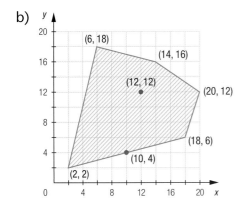

Ordered pair	$z = 7x + 9y$
(2, 2)	
(6, 18)	
(10, 4)	
(12, 12)	
(14, 16)	
(18, 6)	
(20, 12)	

c)

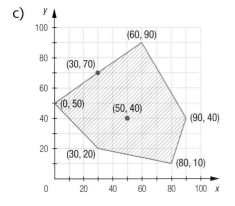

Ordered pair	$z = -1.2x + 0.4y + 2$
(0, 50)	
(30, 20)	
(30, 70)	
(50, 40)	
(60, 90)	
(80, 10)	
(90, 40)	

2 For each of the situations below, do the following:

1) Identify a system of inequalities that represents the constraints.
2) Describe the target objective.
3) Determine the rule of the optimizing function.

a) **Situation 1**

A broadcasting station wants to minimize the cost of a news program that contains sports and national news. The time devoted to sports represents more than 5% and less than 20% of the total length of the program. The time devoted to national news is more than 20 min and does not exceed 35 min. In addition, a maximum of 75 min are allotted to the program. The sports news costs $25/min to produce and the national news, $15/min.

b) **Situation 2**

A company must build airplanes as quickly as possible. A Type-**A** airplane costs $200 million to build and a Type-**B** airplane, $125 million. The company has at most $5 billion to build the airplanes, and there must be at least 5 more Type-**A** airplanes than double the number of Type-**B** airplanes. The company cannot build more than 30 airplanes. It takes 3 weeks to build a Type-**A** airplane and 5 weeks for a Type-**B** airplane.

Like other motorized vehicles, airplanes contribute to global warming. However, over long distances a well-filled airplane does not emit any more greenhouse gasses than an automobile. For example, the *Airbus 380* uses 3 to 4.5 L/100 km for each occupant. Aviation accounts for approximately 3% of all greenhouse gasses.

3 Every week, Marcel works at a theatre and at a shoe store. He can't work more than 45 h/week. He must work more than 15 h at the shoe store and spend at least 60% of his total work time at the theatre. He earns $15/h at the store and $11/h at the theatre.

a) Draw the polygon of constraints associated with this situation.

b) Identify the rule that allows you to calculate Marcel's weekly salary.

c) Below are a few suggestions related to the potential distribution of Marcel's work time:

　❶ 15 h at the store and 30 h at the theatre
　❷ 16 h at the store and 29 h at the theatre
　❸ 17 h at the store and 26 h at the theatre
　❹ 19 h at the store and 26 h at the theatre

Among the suggestions above, determine which one maximizes Marcel's weekly salary while respecting all the constraints.

4 In a textile factory, the weekly contribution to the pension fund is $30 for each full-time employee and $10 for each part-time employee. The rule of the optimizing function is $z = 30x + 10y$.

a) What do the variables x and y represent in this situation?

b) What does the optimizing function allow you to calculate?

c) Using words, provide a constraint that could correspond to each of the following inequalities:

1) $x \geq 0$
2) $y \geq 0$
3) $x + y \leq 240$
4) $x \geq 3y + 25$
5) $x \leq 200$
6) $y \geq 30$

Synthetic textiles are composed of fibres that were selected for their specific characteristics. For example, aramid fibres are heat-resistant and are used in the aerospace industry, for the manufacture of bulletproof clothes or as a substitute for asbestos.

5 An entrepreneur builds houses using Models **A** and **B**; the houses bring in profits of $30,000 and $40,000, respectively. The municipal administration requires that he build at least 30 houses, including a minimum of 8 Model-**A** houses and 12 Model-**B** houses. The number of Model-**B** houses must be at least equal to half the number of Model-**A** houses. In addition, each Model-**A** house contains 8 windows and each Model-**B** house contains 12 windows. However, the entrepreneur can only purchase a maximum of 400 windows.

a) Using variable x to represent the number of Model-**A** houses and variable y to represent the number of Model-**B** houses, determine the rule that allows you to calculate the entrepreneur's profit.

b) Among the points identified on the polygon of constraints below, determine which possesses the coordinates that generate the highest profit.

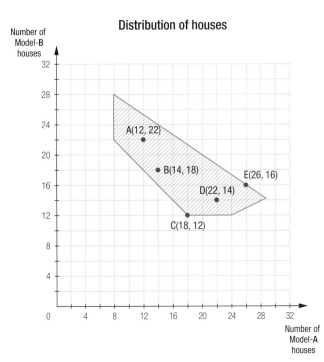

Distribution of houses

Number of Model-B houses

A(12, 22)
B(14, 18)
E(26, 16)
D(22, 14)
C(18, 12)

Number of Model-A houses

There are many types of windows. Be they hung windows, folding windows, Australian windows or hopper windows, each type of window possesses characteristics that are specific to the culture that invented and used it.

6 The adjacent graph displays a polygon of constraints. Determine the rule of the optimizing function such that, among the points identified, the following occurs:

a) The coordinates of point A generate the highest value.

b) The coordinates of point B generate the lowest value.

c) The coordinates of points C and D generate the same value.

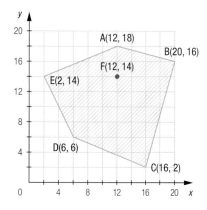

7 A manufacturer of computer products makes computer keyboards and mice. Each keyboard costs $12 to make and sells for $20; each mouse costs $18 to make and sells for $25. This manufacturer must make at least 75 keyboards and 125 mice. The total number of mice produced must be at least 10% greater than the number of keyboards, and the total number of products made must not exceed 350. The polygon of constraints shown below illustrates this situation.

a) Using k to represent the number of keyboards and m, the number of mice, determine the rule of the function that allows you to calculate:

1) the production costs

2) the revenue generated by the sale of the two products

3) the profit generated by the sale of the two products

b) Among the four points identified on the polygon of constraints, identify the one whose coordinates:

1) minimize production costs

2) maximize revenue

3) maximize profit

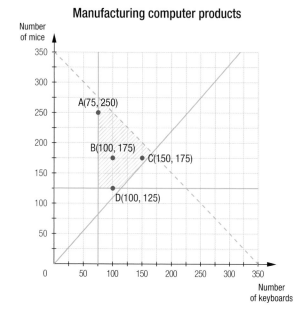

Manufacturing computer products

The ancestor of the mouse is the trackball which, when rotated by the user's fingers, moved the cursor on the screen. The mouse as we know it today was invented in 1968 by Douglas Englebart. However, the trackball is still the preferred tool in some areas of computer-related activities.

8 A company produces bottles of fruit juice in two sizes: small and large. Each small bottle and each large bottle generates a profit of $0.50 and $0.90, respectively. Manufacturing a small bottle requires 150 cm^2 of plastic while manufacturing a large bottle requires 250 cm^2. The company would like its weekly profit to be at least $110 and would like to minimize the amount of plastic used. A maximum of 200 bottles/week can be produced with a minimum of 40 small bottles. The variables s and l respectively represent the number of small and the number of large bottles made each week.

a) What is the target objective in this situation?

b) What is the rule of the optimizing function?

c) Among the points indicated on the polygon of constraints shown below, which represents the most advantageous solution?

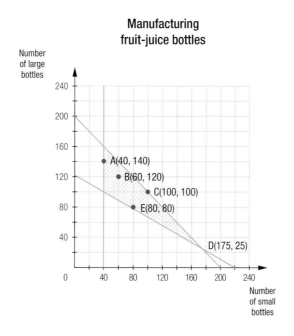

Manufacturing fruit-juice bottles

9 A dairy cooperative earns money from the sale of goat's milk and cow's milk. Goat's milk generates a profit of $0.95/L and cow's milk, a profit of $0.55/L.

a) Define the two variables in this situation.

b) Determine the rule that represents the profit generated by the sale of the two products.

c) Invent three realistic constraints that could be associated with this situation.

Goat's milk is digested much easier than cow's milk. It contains less lactose, approximately 40 g/L, than that of cow's milk which contains approximately 50 g/L. Goat's milk is also used in the production of various types of cheeses, such as feta.

10 a) Among points A, B, C, D and E of the adjacent polygon of constraints, identify the one whose coordinates maximize the function and whose rule is:

1) $z = 4x + 5y$ 2) $z = 7x + 11y$

b) For each of the previous cases, explain why the coordinates of point E cannot maximize the rule.

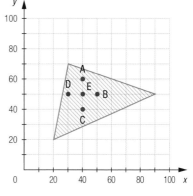

11 Every day, an athlete performs cardiovascular and muscular exercises. This person must spend at least two-thirds of the time doing cardio and at least 15 min on muscular training. This individual's schedule does not allow for more than 90 min of training each day. One min of cardio burns 10 calories and 1 min of muscular training burns 6 calories. This individual would like to burn as many calories as possible.

a) Create the polygon of constraints associated with this situation.

b) What is the rule of the optimizing function?

c) The athlete plans to do 60 min of cardiovascular exercises and 30 min of muscular training. Identify a more advantageous distribution of training time.

d) The individual would now like to burn at least 700 calories while training for as little time as possible. The polygon of constraints shown below represents this situation.

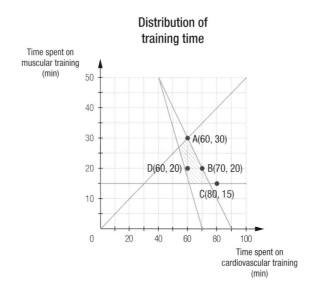

Distribution of training time

1) What type of polygon of constraints is involved?

2) What is the rule of this optimizing function?

3) Among the suggested ordered pairs, which represents a distribution of time that meets the athlete's objective?

12 In an auditorium, lamps with a power of 150 W or 250 W are installed on the ceiling. In order to conserve energy, the total power of these lamps must be as low as possible while respecting the following constraints:

- The number of 150-W lamps must represent at most $\frac{3}{4}$ of the total number of lamps.
- The area of the auditorium's ceiling is 400 m².
- Good lighting requires a power of at least 100 W/m².
- The budget authorized for purchasing these lamps is at most $25,000.
- There are 60 150-W lamps already installed.
- A 150-W lamp costs $70 and a 250-W lamp costs $90.

Identify which of the following options results in the most advantageous solution:

A 90 150-W lamps and 90 250-W lamps

B 100 150-W lamps and 150 250-W lamps

C 60 150-W lamps and 135 250-W lamps

D 240 150-W lamps and 85 250-W lamps

E 65 150-W lamps and 180 250-W lamps

The Sydney Opera House is one of the most famous architectural works of the 20th century. Its shell-inspired design exists in perfect harmony with Sydney's port. The building has also been named a UNESCO World Heritage Site.

This section is related to LES 2 and 3.

PROBLEM Efficient agriculture

A farmer sows a part of his fields with barley and another part with soy. The tables and graph below provide information about this situation.

Barley and soy cultivation

Type of crop	Barley	Soy
Amount of fertilizer needed (kg/hectare)	238	204
Sowing costs ($/hectare)	62	124
Seed yield (tons/hectare)	2	1.5
Profit generated by the sale of the grain ($/ton)	212.50	410

Field cultivation

Total area of fields (hectares)	450
Amount of fertilizer available (kg)	101 150
Capital available for sowing ($)	49,600

The soy is a herbaceous annual plant coming from the southeastern regions of Asia. With respect to major farming crops, soy is the second largest crop in Québec.

Sowing a farmer's fields

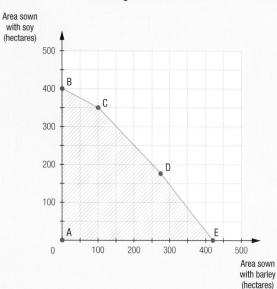

Area sown with soy (hectares) / Area sown with barley (hectares)

What surface area should be sown with barley and soy in order to maximize profit?

A warehouse owner buys new structures to store boxes. Each steel structure can hold 40 boxes, and each iron structure can hold 60 boxes. The owner would like to maximize the number N of boxes to be stored while respecting a set of constraints represented by the adjacent polygon of constraints.

Distribution of steel and iron structures in a warehouse

A(30, 70)

B(70, 50)

C(40, 10)

a. If x represents the number of steel structures and y, the number of iron structures, determine the rule of the optimizing function.

b. Considering the context, provide the meaning of each of the following equations.

1) $2000 = 40x + 60y$ 2) $3500 = 40x + 60y$

3) $5000 = 40x + 60y$ 4) $6500 = 40x + 60y$

Each of the equations given in **b.** are illustrated as a straight line in the graph shown below. These lines can be considered to be parallel paths left by a scanning line travelling from l_1 toward l_4.

c. Explain the significance of the coordinates of points that belong to line l_3 and are located on the polygon of constraints.

d. Determine the slope of the scanning line.

e. Describe how the number of boxes that can be stored varies as the scanning line travels from l_1 to l_4.

f. Explain whether it is possible to respect the constraints and store a total of:

1) 2000 boxes   2) 6500 boxes

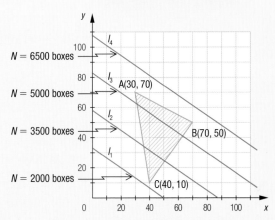

Distribution of steel and iron structures in a warehouse

$N = 6500$ boxes

$N = 5000$ boxes   A(30, 70)

$N = 3500$ boxes

B(70, 50)

$N = 2000$ boxes

C(40, 10)

g. Complete the table below.

Vertex	$40x + 60y$	N
A(30, 70)	▬▬	■
B(70, 50)	▬▬	■
C(40, 10)	▬▬	■

h. Determine the coordinates of the point on the polygon of constraints that allows for the storage of:

1) the maximum number of boxes
2) the minimum number of boxes

Market tendencies force the owner to change the format of the boxes. Now, each steel structure can hold 50 boxes, and each iron structure can hold 100 boxes.

i. What is the rule of this optimizing function?

j. Complete the table below.

Total number of boxes	$N = \blacksquare\, x + \blacksquare\, y$	$y = $
2000	▬ $= \blacksquare\, x + \blacksquare\, y$	$l_5: y = 20 - \dfrac{x}{2}$
4000	▬ $= \blacksquare\, x + \blacksquare\, y$	$l_6: y = $ ▬▬
6000	▬ $= \blacksquare\, x + \blacksquare\, y$	$l_7: y = $ ▬▬
8500	▬ $= \blacksquare\, x + \blacksquare\, y$	$l_8: y = $ ▬▬

The lines associated with the equations obtained above are illustrated in the graph below.

k. What are the coordinates of the point on the polygon of constraints that generates the storage of a minimum number of boxes?

l. Where on the polygon of constraints are the points whose coordinates generate the storage of a maximum number of boxes?

m. When the optimal solution is generated by:

1) the coordinates of a single point, what conjecture can you formulate regarding the position of this point on the polygon of constraints?

2) the coordinates of several points, what conjecture can you formulate regarding the position of these points on the polygon of constraints?

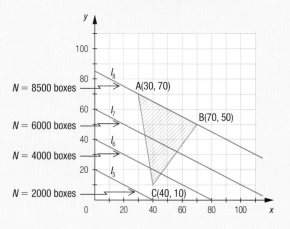

Distribution of steel and iron structures in a warehouse

$N = 8500$ boxes
$N = 6000$ boxes
$N = 4000$ boxes
$N = 2000$ boxes

ACTIVITY 2 Fish farming

A fish-farming operation contracts a company to build trout-raising tanks capable of holding 3 million L of water and salmon-raising tanks capable of holding 5 million L of water. The total number of tanks cannot exceed 16, and the difference between the number of salmon tanks and trout tanks cannot exceed 4. In addition, a total of at least 60 million L of water is needed. A trout tank costs $10,000,000 to build, and a salmon tank costs $14,000,000. This fish farmer must figure out how many tanks of each type to build in order to minimize costs.

a. Define the two variables in this situation.

b. What is the fish-farming operation's objective?

c. What is the rule of the optimizing function?

d. Translate the constraints into a system of inequalities.

e. Draw the polygon of constraints in a Cartesian plane.

f. 1) Find the point on the polygon of constraints whose coordinates generate the optimal value.

   2) What is the optimal value?

g. Provide a recommendation for this fish farmer regarding which tanks should be purchased.

Fish farming is one of the branches of aquaculture which is the aquatic equivalent of agriculture. Fish farmers raise fish in artificial basins or in giant cages placed in the sea or in lakes.

Techno math

A graphing calculator allows you to create and use programs in order to perform certain simulations.

Screen 1   **Screen 2**

This screen allows you to execute, modify or create a new program.

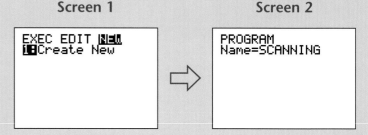

```
EXEC EDIT NEW
1:Create New
```

```
PROGRAM
Name=SCANNING
```

Screen 3   **Screen 4**

These two screens allow you to select certain design or programming instructions. For example, the `Line` instruction allows you to draw a segment from two endpoints.

```
DRAW POINTS STO
1:ClrDraw
2:Line(
3:Horizontal
4:Vertical
5:Tangent(
6:DrawF
7↓Shade(
```

```
CTL I/O EXEC
1:Input
2:Prompt
3:Disp
4:DispGraph
5:DispTable
6:Output(
7↓getKey
```

Screen 5   **Screens 6 and 7**

This screen displays the commands belonging to a program that allows you display a polygon of constraints as well as the movement of a scanning line.

```
PROGRAM:SCANNING
:ClrDraw
:DispGraph
:Disp "OPTIMIZE
"
:Disp "Z=AX+BY"
:Prompt A,B
:-A/B→P
Line(2,4,6,7)
Line(6,7,8,2)
Line(8,2,2,4)
For(Z,1,Ymax+Ym
xabs(P),Yscl)
If P<0:Then
Line(0,Z,Xmax,X
maxP+Z)
:Else
:Line(0,-XmaxP+Z
,Xmax,Z)
:End:Pause :End
```

These screens show the execution of a program using values that were entered.

```
prgmSCANNING
```

```
OPTIMIZE
Z=AX+BY
A=?1
B=?2
```

Screen 8

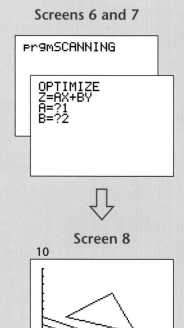

a. Based on the program on Screen **5**, determine the coordinates of the vertices of the polygon of constraints on Screen **8**.

b. Based on Screens **5** to **8**, determine:

1) the rule of the optimizing function   2) the slope of the lines on Screen **8**

3) the ordered pair that generates a maximum   4) the ordered pair that generates a minimum

c. On Screen **7**, what values must be entered for the scanning line to be parallel to the side of the polygon of constraints that is furthest from the origin?

d. Use the SCANNING program to identify the ordered pair that generates:

1) the maximum of the function whose rule is $z = 3x + 2y$

2) the minimum of the function whose rule is $z = 5x - 4y$

LINEAR PROGRAMMING AND OPTIMAL SOLUTIONS

Linear programming is a field of study that examines optimization problems by using first-degree inequalities and equations.

Solving an optimization problem entails searching for a solution that generates a maximum or a minimum of the optimizing function while taking various constraints and the target objective into account. The solution can take on two forms:

- The optimal solution is generated by the coordinates of a single point on the polygon of constraints. This point is usually a vertex of the polygon.

- The optimal solution is generated by the coordinates of several points on the polygon of constraints. These points usually belong to a side of the polygon.

SOLVING AN OPTIMIZATION PROBLEM

There are different ways of solving an optimization problem. For an optimizing function whose rule is $z = ax + by + c$, note the following:

- The line whose slope is $-\frac{a}{b}$ and that travels across the Cartesian plan is called a scanning line.

  Using this line allows you to graphically locate the point or points on the polygon of constraints whose coordinates generate the optimal value.

- Evaluating this function at each of the vertices of the polygon of constraints allows you to determine which ones have coordinates that generate the optimal value.

E.g. 1)

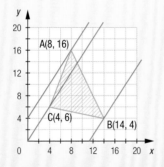

Vertex	$z = 3x - 2y$
A(8, 16)	$z = 3 \times 8 - 2 \times 16 = {-8}$
B(14, 4)	$z = 3 \times 14 - 2 \times 4 = 34$
C(4, 6)	$z = 3 \times 4 - 2 \times 6 = 0$

- The coordinates of point A minimize the optimizing function.

- The coordinates of point B maximize the optimizing function.

2)

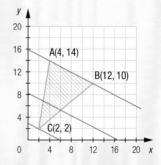

Vertex	$z = 3x + 6y$
A(4, 14)	$z = 3 \times 4 + 6 \times 14 = 96$
B(12, 10)	$z = 3 \times 12 + 6 \times 10 = 96$
C(2, 2)	$z = 3 \times 2 + 6 \times 2 = 18$

- Since the coordinates of vertices A and B both generate the maximum value of the optimizing function, the coordinates of all points located on the segment AB maximize the function.

- The coordinates of point C minimize the optimizing function.

An optimizing problem can be solved in the following way.	E.g. A car manufacturer that builds compact cars and minivans wishes to maximize its weekly profit. The profit generated is $4,000 for each compact car and $10,000 for each minivan. The manufacturer's weekly production capacity is 2100 vehicles at most, and it must build at least 1000 compact cars and at least 200 minivans each week. The number of compact cars built must be at least twice as many as the number of minivans built.
1. Define the two variables.	The variable x represents the number of compact cars, and the variable y represents the number of minivans.
2. Determine the target objective and identify the rule of the optimizing function.	The car manufacturer's target objective is to maximize its weekly profit ($ in thousands), which can be calculated by means of the function $P = 4x + 10y$.
3. Translate the constraints into a system of inequalities.	$x + y \leq 2100$ $x \geq 1000$ $y \geq 200$ $x \geq 2y$
4. Draw the polygon of constraints in a Cartesian plane.	**Distribution of a car manufacturer's production** Number of minivans A(1400, 700) D(1000, 500) C(1000, 200) B(1900, 200) Number of compact cars
5. Identify the point or points whose coordinates generate the optimal value.	By using a scanning line or by substituting the coordinates of each of the vertices for the variables x and y in the optimizing function, you determine that the point associated with vertex A(1400, 700) generate the maximum profit.
6. Find the ordered-pair solution(s) and the optimal value, considering the context.	The manufacturer must build 1400 compact cars and 700 minivans each week, generating a maximum profit of $12.6 million.

practice 1.4

1 In each of the graphs below, a polygon of constraints and a scanning line have been drawn. For each case, identify the point or points whose coordinates generate:

1) the minimum value of the optimizing function

2) the maximum value of the optimizing function

a)

Optimizing function:
$$z = x + y$$

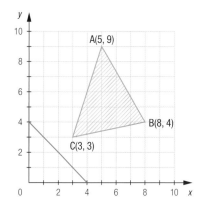

b)

Optimizing function:
$$z = 3x - 10y$$

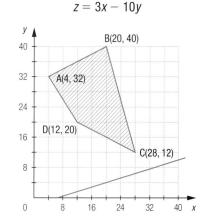

c)

Optimizing function:
$$z = x - 2y$$

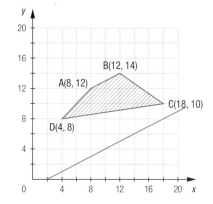

d)

Optimizing function:
$$z = 2x + y$$

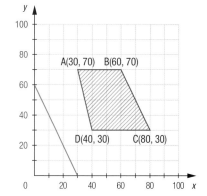

2 The vertices of a polygon of constraints are A(10, 12), B(40, 60), C(62, 54) and D(50, 15). Identify the vertex whose coordinates generate:

a) the maximum of the optimizing function whose rule is $z = 3x + 12y$

b) the minimum of the optimizing function whose rule is $z = 0.8x - 2y$

3 A polygon of constraints is shown in the adjacent graph, and the rules of two optimizing functions are provided below.

① $z_1 = 2x + 3y$
   Objective: maximize

② $z_2 = 5x - 4y$
   Objective: minimize

For each of these functions, do the following:

a) Determine the point or points whose coordinates generate the function's optimal value.

b) Calculate this optimal value.

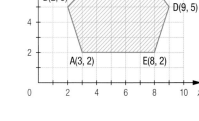

4 Considering the adjacent polygon of constraints, for each case, identify:

1) the maximum of the optimizing function
2) the minimum of the optimizing function

a) $z = 3x - 4y$ b) $z = 0.5x + y$

c) $z = 11x - 2y$ d) $z = -x - 0.1y$

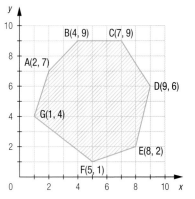

5 For each case, determine the coordinates of the point or points whose coordinates generate the optimizing function's maximum.

a) Optimizing function:
   $z = 0.5x - 0.1y$

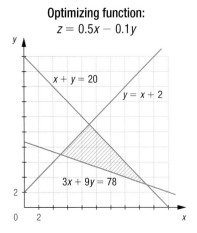

b) Optimizing function:
   $z = 3x + 4y$

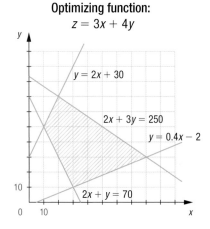

c) Optimizing function:
   $z = 0.3x + 0.5y$

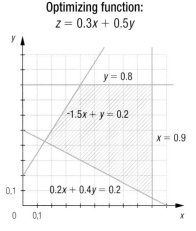

d) Optimizing function:
   $z = 13x - 10y$

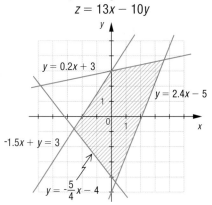

6 For each case, determine the coordinates of the point or points that meet the objective indicated.

a) **Objective:** maximize
Optimizing function: $z = 2x + 3y$
Constraints:
$$x \geq 0$$
$$y \geq 0$$
$$x + y \leq 5$$
$$y \leq x$$

b) **Objective:** minimize
Optimizing function: $z = 10x - 4y$
Constraints: $x \geq 1$
$$y \geq 20$$
$$y \leq 2x + 5$$
$$y \leq -0.6x + 50$$

7 Based on the polygon of constraints below, determine the rule of an optimizing function such that each of the following occurs:

a) The coordinates of point A generate a minimum of the function.

b) The coordinates of the points located on segment CD generate a maximum of the function.

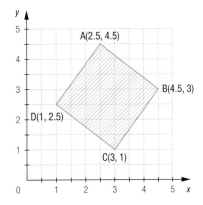

8 Each of the polygons of constraints below is associated with a situation in which only the points whose coordinates are integers need to be considered. For each case, determine the coordinates of the point or points that minimize the optimizing function.

a) **Optimizing function:**
$$z = 3x - 2.5y$$

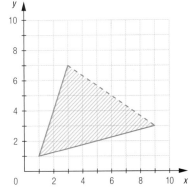

b) **Optimizing function:**
$$z = 2x + 3y$$

9 A farmer owns an orchard with a surface area of 900 m² on which he grows apple trees and pear trees. Each tree produces either 100 kg of apples or 80 kg of pears each year. Apples sell for $5/kg and pears sell for $6/kg. The area allotted to each apple tree is 3 m², and the area allotted to each pear tree is 2 m². The farmer grows at least 100 trees of each type and cannot harvest more than 32 800 kg of fruit.

a) Define each of the variables.

b) Determine the rule of the optimizing function.

In botany, pears and apples are considered false fruits because they do not develop the way most fruits do.

c) Represent the constraints using a system of inequalities.

d) Draw the polygon of constraints in a Cartesian plane.

e) Determine the coordinates of the point or points that generate the optimal value.

f) How many trees of each type must the farmer plant to meet the target objective?

g) How much revenue should the farmer anticipate?

10 For a field trip, a school's administration rents 20-seat buses and 45-seat buses. Its objective is to maximize the number of students that can be transported while respecting the constraints illustrated by the polygon of constraints below.

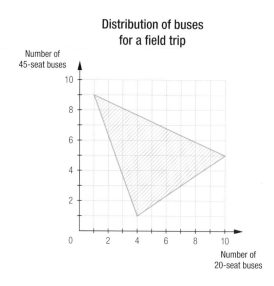

Distribution of buses for a field trip

Number of 45-seat buses / Number of 20-seat buses

a) Determine the rule of the optimizing function.

b) Explain why, in this context, only points whose coordinates are whole numbers need to be considered.

c) How many ordered pairs allow the administration to meet its objective?

d) What is the maximum number of students that can take part in the field trip?

11 A wave pool cannot accommodate more than 150 people, including a maximum of 90 children. The ratio of $\dfrac{\text{number of adults}}{\text{number of children}}$ must not be less than $\dfrac{1}{2}$. The number N of lifeguards is determined by the rule $N = \dfrac{x}{10} + \dfrac{y}{15}$ where x represents the number of children and y represents the number of adults in the wave pool.

a) Determine the number of children and the number of adults that require the presence of a maximum number of lifeguards.

b) Determine this maximum number of lifeguards.

12 SUPERCOMPUTER The computing speed of a supercomputer is measured in FLOPS. For example, a supercomputer that achieves 5 teraFLOPS can perform 5 billion operations every second. A military research department wants to acquire a set of supercomputers. Below are the characteristics of two models:

Model	A	B
Cost ($ in millions)	20	24
Computing speed (teraFLOPS)	40	60
Floor space required (m^2)	5	10

The space available for storing the computers is 240 m^2. How many computers of each type should the department buy if the target objective is to:

a) maximize computing speed while respecting a maximum budget of $800 million?

b) minimize expenses while obtaining a minimum total computing speed of 480 teraFLOPS?

The first supercomputer, the Cray-1, was designed in 1976. It was capable of performing 100 million operations/s. IBM's Roadrunner, designed in 2008, can achieve a petaFLOPS (Floating-Point Operations Per Second), a computing capacity one million times greater than that of the Cray-1. Supercomputers are used mainly for research in fields such as climatology and molecular biology.

13 A company makes screws and bolts in Workshops **A** and **B**. The following is information regarding production in each of the workshops:

- The machining time for a screw is 2 min in Workshop **A** and 4 min in Workshop **B**.
- The machining time for a bolt is 3 min in Workshop **A** and 2 min in Workshop **B**.
- Workshop **A** is available 168 h/week.
- Workshop **B** is available 200 h/week.
- The number of screws made in each workshop is identical.
- The number of bolts made in each workshop is identical.

The profit generated by each screw is $0.18, and $0.20 is generated for each bolt. How many screws and bolts must the company make each week in order to maximize its revenue?

14 A taxi cooperative would like to purchase at least 10 hybrid vehicles in addition to at least 20 conventional vehicles. To be competitive, this cooperative must have a fleet of at least 60 vehicles. The daily fuel consumption of a conventional vehicle is 30 L/day; that of a hybrid vehicle is only 18 L/day. However, a hybrid vehicle costs $20/day in maintenance, and a conventional vehicle costs $15/day. A conventional vehicle sells for $18,000 and a hybrid vehicle for $26,000. The price of gas is $1.10/L. This cooperative has obtained a $2,000,000 loan to buy all its vehicles. The cooperative's manager must minimize the daily costs associated with running and maintaining the fleet of taxis.

What is the number of hybrid vehicles and conventional vehicles that will allow the manager to reach this target objective?

Taxi boat that travels from Granville to downtown Vancouver.

Floating taxi that is tied to a loading dock in the Maldives, an island located in the Indian Ocean.

15 The polygon of constraints shown below is associated with the following system of inequalities.

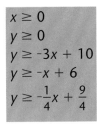

$$x \geq 0$$
$$y \geq 0$$
$$y \geq -3x + 10$$
$$y \geq -x + 6$$
$$y \geq -\frac{1}{4}x + \frac{9}{4}$$

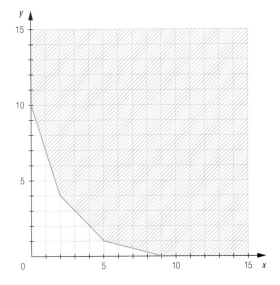

a) What type of polygon of constraints is this?

b) Draw a scanning line associated with the function whose rule is $z = 4x + 5y$.

c) What are the coordinates of the point that minimizes this function?

d) Is it possible to find a point whose coordinates maximize this function? Explain your answer.

16 In order to treat a patient, a doctor decides to administer a treatment combining Medications **A** and **B**. The side effects associated with these medications force the doctor to respect the following constraints:

- The dosage x of Medication **A** must be at least 5 mg without exceeding 15 mg.

- The dosage y of Medication **B** must be at least 8 mg without exceeding 25 mg.

- The total dosage of medication produced cannot exceed 35 mg.

- The dosage of Medication **A** must represent at most 40% of the total dosage of medication produced.

The desired effects of this treatment can be quantified using an efficiency index z between 0 and 1 that is calculated by means of the function $z = 0.0305x + 0.025y$.

a) 1) Determine the quantity of each type of medication to be administered so that the efficiency index is as high as possible.

2) Calculate the value of the efficiency index in this case.

b) If Medication **A** can only be taken in the form of 2.5-mg tablets and Medication **B** can only be taken in the form of 5-mg tablets, do the following:

1) Determine the number of tablets of each medication to be taken so that the efficiency index is as high as possible.

2) Calculate the value of the efficiency index in this case.

A large number of Canada's bio-pharmaceutical industries are found in Québec, mostly in Montréal, thanks to many international pharmaceutical companies.

George Dantzig

His youth

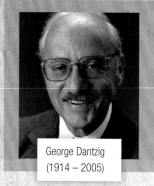

George Dantzig
(1914 – 2005)

Born in the United States on November 8, 1914, George Bernard Dantzig was the son of Russian mathematician Tobias Dantzig. As a high-school student, George Dantzig was fascinated by geometry. His father encouraged this passion by frequently giving him complex geometric problems to solve.

An extraordinary anecdote

It is told that Dantzig, upon arriving late to a class one day, noticed that there were two problems up on the board. Thinking that the problems were homework, he solved them and submitted them to his professor a few days later. It was only then that he realized that they were examples of statistical problems that had previously never been solved. This anecdote inspired one of the scenes in the American film *Good Will Hunting*.

Studies interrupted by the war

Midway through his doctoral studies, Dantzig was forced to interrupt his studies by World War II when he spent his time at the U.S. Air Force Office of Statistical Control. After this conflict, he completed his doctorate, which he received in 1946.

Linear programming

As an adviser to the Federal Aviation Administration, George Dantzig was charged with increasing the speed and efficiency of deployment planning, training and logistical support for combat units. At the time, the term "programming" referred to the organization of this kind of military operation.

Following is a simplified example of what could have been presented to Dantzig. A situation requires the deployment of 3500 to 5000 soldiers. Of these, some are infantry, and the rest are artillery. At least 2000 infantrymen and at least 1000 artillerymen must be deployed, and the number of artillerymen must not exceed the number of infantrymen. Considering that infantrymen and artillerymen could not be deployed simultaneously, Dantzig had to find the means to execute this deployment with minimal time and resources.

In fulfilling this mandate, Dantzig developed a method, called the "simplex method" which allowed problems involving a very large number of constraints and variables that could be translated into a system of first-degree inequalities to be solved using matrices. Today, Dantzig is considered the father of linear programming, which is optimization involving systems of first-degree inequalities and equations.

3-D optimization

When the number of variables involved in a linear programming problem is equal to 3, the graphical representation of the system of inequalities corresponds to a polyhedron of constraints. When the number of variables is greater than 3, a hyperpolyhedron or a polytope of constraints is required.

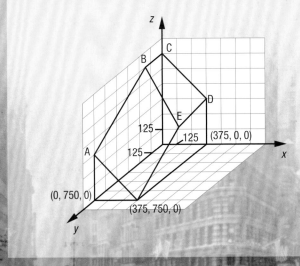

1. In the troop deployment example, if the deployment of 500 infantrymen takes 24 h and that of 500 artillerymen takes 48 h:

a) how many infantrymen and artillerymen can be deployed in minimum time?

b) what is the minimum number of days in which the deployment can be executed?

c) what is the maximum amount of time that can be dedicated to this operation?

d) how many infantrymen and artillerymen are deployed when the maximum time is dedicated?

2. In relation to the polyhedron of constraints:

a) provide the non-negative constraints

b) determine the coordinates of:

1) vertex A

2) vertex C

3) vertex D

In the workplace

Logisticians specializing in humanitarian aid

Their role

Humanitarian aid is generally aimed at poorer populations, at inhabitants of a disaster area or at innocent people affected by war. This aid, which is often intended to meet vital needs, can take on various forms: transportation and distribution of food staples, organization of health care and development of a system for the distribution of drinking water. Depending on the scope and type of needs, logisticians specializing in humanitarian aid can be called upon to organize emergency or permanent aid.

One of the most-decorated Canadian soldiers, Lieutenant-General Roméo A. Dallaire is best known for having acted in a humanitarian capacity during the genocide committed by Hutu extremists in Rwanda. Among his decorations are the Order of Canada, the Order of Military Merit, the National Order of Québec and the Legion of Merit of the United States.

Doing more with less

Logisticians specializing in humanitarian aid have to deal with a multitude of constraints related to time, space and resources. In short, they have to deliver a maximum of items in a minimum of time and space in order to help as many people as possible, and they must often do so despite very limited material resources.

Unique needs

Humanitarian crises are not all the same. For example, some are caused by natural catastrophes and others by armed conflicts. Also, because of the large number of factors involved, populations that have been affected by disasters differ from one situation to another. That is why logisticians specializing in humanitarian aid must first evaluate the victims' specific needs in order to identify the type of resources needed. After that, these logisticians must maximize the use of transportation, bearing in mind the potentially difficult conditions such as impassable roads and downed communications.

From emergency humanitarian aid to long-term humanitarian aid

Once the urgent basic needs have been met, the logisticians specializing in humanitarian aid must then arrange more long-term aid while the victims rebuild their community and regain their independence in a safe environment.

The table below shows the evolution of the needs of people who have been affected by a disaster, based on the amount of time elapsed since the beginning of the humanitarian crisis.

Evolution of the needs of disaster victims

Period of humanitarian crisis	Week 1	Week 2	Week 3
Needs	Food and water	Food, water and 50 boxes of medicine	Food, water and 100 boxes of equipment

In providing aid, the logisticians also had to consider the following information:

- The mass of a box of food is 15 kg.
- The mass of a tank of water is 25 kg.
- The mass of a box of medicine is 15 kg.
- The mass of a box of equipment is 50 kg.
- The amount of water delivered cannot be less than twice the mass of the food delivered.

1. If there are 5 trucks available to transport a load that is no more than 3500 kg or 150 boxes, what is the maximum amount of each type of supply that can be delivered to a disaster area for each of the 3 weeks following the start of the humanitarian crisis?

overview

1 Graphically represent each of the systems of inequalities below.

a) $y > 3x - 2$

$y > -2x - 5$

b) $y \geq 2$

$y < 4x + 2$

c) $y \geq -\dfrac{3}{2}x - 3$

$5x - 4y + 7 \geq 0$

d) $-4x + 7y > 2$

$12x - 8y \leq 1$

2 For each case, determine the system of inequalities that represents the solution sets shown below.

a)

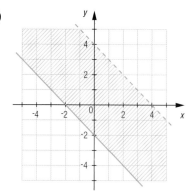

b)

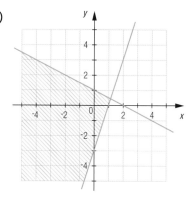

c)

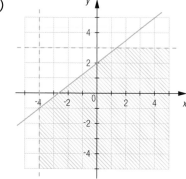

d)

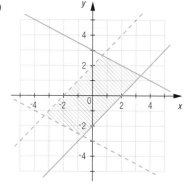

3 For each case, represent the system of inequalities in a Cartesian plane, and determine the coordinates of the vertices of the resulting polygon of constraints.

a) $x \geq 0$
$y \geq 0$
$-x + 2y \leq 0$
$2x + y \geq 6$
$x + 2y \leq 7$

b) $x \geq 0$
$y \geq 0$
$y \geq -x + 2$
$y \leq -3x + 6$
$y \leq 2x + 2$

c) $x \geq 0$
$y \geq 0$
$2x + 3y \geq 20$
$4x + y \geq 10$
$x - 4y \leq 0$

d) $x \geq 20$
$y \geq 0$
$12x + 20y \geq 800$
$y \geq 1.5x - 80$
$x + y \leq 100$

4 From ordered pairs A(-1, -6), B(2, 7), C(3, 4), D(-10, -20) and E(1, -16), determine which one(s) are a solution to:

a) System of inequalities ①

b) System of inequalities ②

c) Systems of inequalities ① and ②

System of inequalities ①
$x \le 4$
$y \ge -12$
$-3x + 4y \le 15$
$2x - y \le 7$

System of inequalities ②
$x \ge y$
$y \le 2x + 7$
$-2x + y < 0$

5 For each case, do the following:

1) Determine the system of inequalities associated with the polygon of constraints.

2) Determine the coordinates of vertex D of the polygon of constraints.

3) Identify the vertices whose coordinates are solutions to the system of inequalities.

a)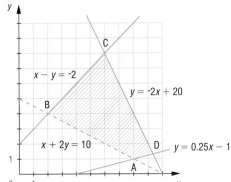

b)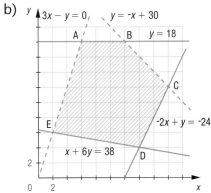

6 From the system of inequalities below, which ones are represented by a polygon of constraints that is not bounded?

A $y \ge -x + 10$
$y \ge -2x + 15$
$x \ge 0$
$y \ge 0$

B $y \le 0.6x + 16$
$y \le 7x - 80$
$x \le 30$
$y \ge -x$

C $-4x + y \le 0$
$4x + 2y \le 20$
$x \ge 0$
$y \ge 0$
$y \le 5$

D $y \le 4x$
$y \le 2x + 10$
$x \ge 0$
$y \ge 0$

7 Following is a system of inequalities:

$$y \ge x - 3$$
$$y \le -0.5x + 5$$
$$y \le 4x - 5$$

How many ordered-pair solutions are there for this system if you consider that:

a) the ordered pairs formed are real numbers?

b) only the ordered pairs formed are whole numbers?

8 For each of the following optimizing functions, do the following:

1) Determine the point(s) of the polygon of constraints whose coordinates generate a maximum.

2) Calculate the maximum value.

a) $z = x + y$

b) $z = 2x - 3y$

c) $z = 0.7x + 0.9y$

d) $z = 0.9x + 0.7y$

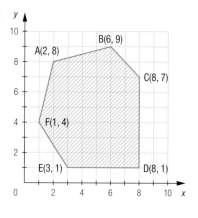

9 For each of the following situations, do the following:

1) Represent the constraints using a system of inequalities.

2) Determine the rule of the optimizing function.

a) A company makes wood chairs and wood stools. Each chair sold yields $20 in profit, and each stool sold yields $12 in profit. Each week, the company makes at least 150 chairs, at least 100 stools and at least double the number of chairs as stools. The total number of chairs and stools made is less than or equal to 1000. The company wants to maximize its profit.

b) An art gallery hires a maximum of 14 full-time or part-time employees. Each part-time employee works 14 h/week, and each full-time employee works 30 h/week. The total number of hours worked by all the employees is less than or equal to 400 hours. Each part-time employee earns $12/h, and each full-time employee earns $14/h. The art gallery wants to minimize its expenses.

From the Canadian Museum of Civilization, this Nuxalk painting on wood depicts a whale and a human form.

10 A bag with a volume of 1 m³ cannot support a mass that is greater than 2650 g. The bag is filled with small cubes made of metal and others of wood; the characteristics of these cubes are shown below.

Presuming that there is no loss of space when the cubes are in the bag, calculate the maximum number of cubes that can be placed in the bag.

Mass: 50 g
Volume: 0.008 m³

Mass: 30 g
Volume: 0.024 m³

"The knapsack problem" is a well-known problem based on linear programming. It can serve as a way of solving certain problems related to transportation and warehousing.

11 A publishing company wants to print a magazine that has colour and black-and-white pages. Each colour page costs $0.07 to produce, and each black-and-white page costs $0.04.

Below are the constraints for the printing of this magazine:

① The magazine has to have a minimum of 45 pages and a maximum of 60 pages.

② The magazine has to have a minimum of 25 colour pages and a maximum of 35 black-and-white pages.

③ The number of colour pages has to represent at most $\frac{3}{8}$ of the total number of pages.

④ The printing costs cannot exceed $3 for each magazine.

a) Represent the constraints with inequalities.

b) Explain why it is impossible to print a magazine that respects all of the constraints provided.

c) Modify the Constraint ③ so that is possible to print the magazine.

12 Two types of machines produce the same metallic piece. Machine **A** produces 9 pieces/min, and Machine **B** produces 7 pieces/min. Machine **A** costs $200,000, and Machine **B** costs $120,000. A factory allots a maximum of $1.84 million to buy this type of machine and wants to purchase at least 12 machines while maximizing production speed.

a) Of the graphs shown below, which one illustrates the polygon of constraints and scanning line associated with this situation?

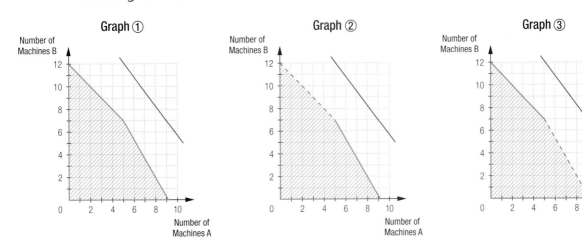

b) Explain why, in this situation, the point whose coordinates represent the optimal solution is not a vertex of the polygon of constraints.

c) Calculate:
   1) the number of machines of each type that will generate the optimal value
   2) the speed of the maximum production

13 Complete the following table.

System of inequalities representing the constraints	$y \le -x + 15$ $y \le 2x - 6$ $-x + 3y \ge -60$	$x \ge 0$ $y \ge 0$ $y \le 15$ $x \le 14$ $y \le 2x + 4$	$y \ge -x - 2$ $y \le x + 4$ $y \le -3x + 8$
Rule of the optimizing function	$z = 0.5x + 2y$	$z = y - 3x$	$z = -10x - 14y$
Target objective	Maximize	Minimize	Maximize
Ordered-pair solution			
Optimal value			

14 The area of a rectangle is at least 100 cm². This constraint can be represented by inequality $L \ge \dfrac{100}{w}$ where L is the length of the rectangle and w is the width.

The adjacent graph represents this inequality:

You are looking for a rectangle that respects the constraints and has the smallest perimeter.

a) Determine the rule of the optimizing function.

b) On this graph, draw the scanning line associated to this function.

c) Graphically determine the coordinates of the point that generates the minimum of the optimizing function.

d) What type of quadrilateral is represented by the ordered pair found in **c)**?

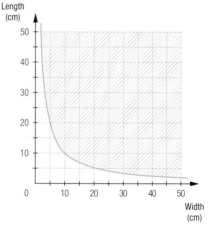

Dimensions of a rectangle whose area is at least 100 cm²

15 A restaurant has small tables that seat 4 people and large tables that seat 6 people. The respective cost for each table is $350 and $450. The restaurant has to have between 60 and 90 seats. The number of small tables has to correspond to at least half and at most three-quarters of the total number of tables. The restaurant wants to minimize the costs associated with the purchase of the tables.

a) Represent each of the constraints with an inequality.

b) What is the target objective?

c) What is the rule of the optimizing function?

d) Represent the polygon of constraints in a Cartesian plane.

e) Determine the number of small tables and large tables that would allow the restaurant to achieve its objective.

f) What is the total cost for purchasing the tables in this case?

16 A city's public transportation service plans to set up a subway service and install two different subway trains that will circulate simultaneously. Following is some information about this subject:

The network cannot support more than 31 trains running simultaneously. How many trains of each type should this city buy if the city's objective is:

Model	Train A	Train B
Cost ($ in millions)	60	68
Number of cars	6	5
Number of passengers for each car	45	60

a) to maximize the number of passengers simultaneously using the subway while respecting the budget of $1.74 billion?

b) to minimize costs for the simultaneous transport of at least 8520 passengers?

17 In order to provide Stores **A** and **B** with a daily supply of fruits and vegetables, a wholesaler sets up a distribution centre. The diagram below contains information about this subject.

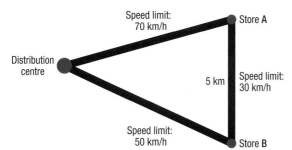

Following are certain constraints related to this situation:

- The distance between Store **A** and the distribution centre is at most 8 km.
- The distance between Store **B** and the distribution centre at most 5 km.
- The sum of the two distances is at least 6 km.
- The distance that separates Store **A** from the distribution centre is at least equal to and at most twice the distance that separates Store **B** from the distribution centre.
- Presume that the delivery truck always follows the speed limit.

The wholesaler wants to minimize the time necessary to do a route.

a) At what distance from Store **A** and Store **B** should the distribution centre be built in order to attain the objective if during a route:

   1) the truck goes from the distribution centre to Store **A**, from Store **A** to Store **B** and from Store **B** to the distribution centre?

   2) the truck goes from the distribution centre to Store **A**, from Store **A** to the distribution centre, from the distribution centre to Store **B** and from Store **B** to the distribution centre?

b) Which of the two proposed routes above represents the optimal solution?

18 The live memory and the processor are two computer components that affect a computer's performance. Saïd is having a customized computer assembled with the following characteristics.

- The processor's speed: a minimum of 1.2 GHz
- Amount of RAM (Random Access Memory): a minimum of 2 MHz
- $\dfrac{\text{amount of RAM}}{\text{the processor's speed}}$: a maximum of 3.2 MHz/GHz

The processor's cost is $100/GHz and the cost of the RAM is $60/MHz. If m represents the amount of RAM (in MHz) and s represents the processor speed (in GHz), the computer's performance index is be expressed by the rule $I = 0.15m + 0.2s$.

Determine the characteristics of a computer for each of the following:

a) a computer that offers the best performance index if Saïd wants to pay no more than $400 for these two components

b) the most economical computer if Saïd wants a performance index of at least 0.7

19 If x and y respectively represent the number of bags of peanuts and the number of bottles of juice sold at a convenience store, express the following constraints in words.

a) $x \geq 0$

b) $y \geq 0$

c) $x + y \leq 90$

d) $y \geq x + 15$

e) $2x \geq 3y$

f) $x + y \geq 60$

20 In the graphs below, each orange curve defines the feasible region of a system of constraints, and the green curve represents a scanning curve associated to a optimizing function.

a) Optimizing function:
$z = 3x + 2y$

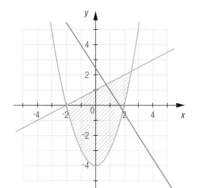

b) Optimizing function:
$z = x^2 + y$

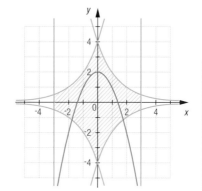

Non-linear programming occurs when at least one of the constraints cannot be expressed by a linear inequality or when the optimizing function cannot be expressed by a linear equation.

Graphically determine the coordinates or points that result in a value that is:

1) maximum

2) minimum

21 As shown below, a 1-dm wide edging is installed around an liquid crystal display (LCD) screen during manufacture.

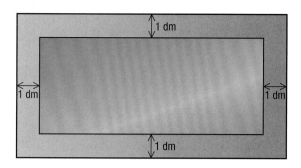

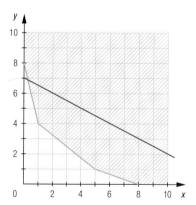

The screen's dimensions, without edging, must respect the following constraints.

The latest generation of screens resemble supple sheets of plastic which can be used to make, among other things, digital books. A new manufacturing process allows for mass production from rolls of plastic, on which pixels have been printed with an ink-jet printer especially made for this process. In addition, the latest generation of screens is actually manufactured in printing shops.

- The ratio of length to width must be at most 16:9 and at least 4:3.

- The length must be at least 24 dm and no more than 35 dm.

Determine the dimensions of the screen, without edging, that requires the least amount of plastic to make its edging.

22 Julianne states that a polygon of constraints is inevitably convex. Is she right? Explain your answer.

23 The adjacent graph displays a polygon of constraints and the scanning line associated with the optimizing function.

a) Write a system of inequalities associated with this polygon of constraints.

b) Determine the rule of the optimizing function.

c) Describe a context that could represent this polygon of constraints and this optimizing function.

24 Create an optimization problem that respects the following conditions.

- The polygon of constrains is bounded.

- The only points of the polygon of constraints that are solutions are coordinates that are whole numbers.

- The target objective is to maximize the optimizing function.

- Many ordered-pair solutions fulfill the objective.

bank of problems

1 A grocer wants to install a minimum of two electronic cash registers and hire at least 16 cashiers. Each cashier earns $350/week. The cost associated with the purchase and maintenance of an electronic cash register is $200/week. The grocer foresees a total budget of at most $7,000/week for these two types of expenses. There cannot be more than 4 cashiers working on one cash register. If h represents the number of cashiers hired and c, the number of cash registers installed, the rule $T = 20 - (0.6h + 0.3c)$ allows you to calculate a client's waiting time T (in min).

What ratio of cash registers to cashiers will allow for a minimal waiting time?

Electronic cash registers help to optimize the flow of customers through a supermarket.

2 Below are statements made by four students which describe the adjacent system.

$$x > 3$$
$$x < 10$$
$$y > {-4}$$
$$y < 15$$
$$2x + 3y < 60$$
$$2x + 3y > 0$$
$$5x - 4y = 15$$

Kevin
The graphical representation of the solution set of this system is an unbounded polygon of constraints.

Melissa
The solution set is comprised of ordered pairs associated with all the points between the two parallel lines.

Minh
The solution set is comprised of all the ordered pairs that satisfy the equation of a line whose slope is positive.

Florence
The solution set is the empty set.

Which student is correct? Explain your answer.

3 Below is information on two types of cabinets made by a furniture manufacturer:

Type of cabinet	Maple cabinet	Oak cabinet
Minimum monthly output	100 cabinets	40 cabinets
Cost of manufacturing one cabinet ($)	200	350
Selling price of one cabinet ($)	400	525
Maximum monthly output	180 cabinets	

Show that the ordered pair that results in maximum revenue does not result in maximum profit.

4 An artisan makes sculptures and pots. The polygons of constraint shown below represent certain restrictions related to the production of these two items.

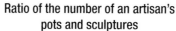

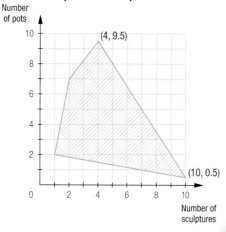

Each sculpture requires 3 h of work while each pot requires 2.5 h of work. The profit from the sale of a sculpture is $75 and that from a pot is $50.

Considering that all the sculptures and all the pots produced will be sold, advise the artisan as to the most advantageous ratio of sculptures to pots to produce.

Steatite, also known as soapstone, is a soft rock that is mainly composed of talc. Due to its soft surface, it is commonly used in sculptures. It is the main material used by Inuit artists. Their work generally represents themes that are associated to their culture: wildlife, scenes from daily life and traditional legends.

5 An alloy is composed of Metal **A** and Metal **B**. Below is some information on this subject:

Composition of Metal A

	Copper	Iron	Zinc	Impurities
Concentration (%)	1	20	25	12

Composition of Metal B

	Copper	Iron	Zinc	Impurities
Concentration (%)	0.2	40	1	23

Composition of the alloy

	Copper	Iron	Zinc
Concentration (%)	Less than or equal to 0.5	Greater than or equal to 34	Greater than or equal to 4

Below are the characteristics of one item made with this alloy:

• The concentration of impurities is minimal.

• The mass of the item is 8 kg.

What quantities (in kg) of Metal **A** and Metal **B** are required to make this item?

In the automobile industry, alloy metals are used for many purposes. The main purposes include the improvement of the durability of the steel frame in case of an accident and the reduction of the mass of the vehicle to reduce gas consumption.

6 A company wishing to market a new multimedia player surveys children between 12 and 17 years of age. Below are the results of this survey:

• The player must be able to support at least 500 audio files and at least 250 video files.

• The player must not support more than a total of 2000 files.

• With this type of player, the number of audio files is generally at least 3 times more than the number of video files.

• Each audio file takes up 3 Mb of memory and each video file, 20 Mb.

• The selling price of the player must be less or equal to $250.

According to this company's marketing specialists, it is possible to determine the selling price p (in $) of this player using the rule $p = 0.02e$ where e represents the available memory (in Mb). In addition the number n of players sold can be determined using the rule $n = 100\ 000 - 120p$.

Determine the total amount of memory available and the selling price for a player that will allow the company to maximize the number of players sold.

The head of a SME that is specialized in the construction of doors and windows receives a report containing the graph and information shown below.

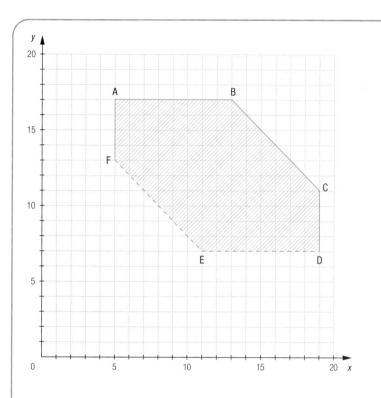

x: daily production of doors (units/day)

y: daily production of windows (units/day)

p: profit (in $)

Equations of the boundary lines

$y = 17$

$x + y = 30$

$x = 19$

$y = 7$

$x + y = 18$

$x = 5$

- If the rule of the optimizing function is $p = 40x + 75y$, the coordinates of point B define the optimal solution.

- If the rule of the optimizing function is $p = 75x + 40y$, the coordinates of point C define the optimal solution.

Write up a report for the head of the SME, and include each of the constraints, each of the rules that correspond to the optimizing functions and the interpretation of the optimal solutions associated with this situation.

The Kennedy Space Center in Florida has the highest door in the world. At a height of 139 m, it provides an access between the launch pad and the orbiter when it is in a vertical position. This door is composed of an upper part, which is itself composed of 7 doors that open vertically. The lower part of this door is composed of 4 doors that open horizontally. The mass of the door is so great that a special mechanism is required to keep it open.

VISI2N

Geometric transformations and equivalent figures

How do you maximize a tent's inhabitable space while using as little canvas as possible to make it? How are geometric transformations involved in designing video games? How do you determine the ideal shape of a container? Many human activities rely on geometry and the optimization of surfaces and space. In "Vision 2," you will perform geometric transformations in a Cartesian plane, and you will identify transformation rules that define the relationship between an initial figure and its image. You will also design objects with the intent of saving materials and optimizing the space occupied.

Arithmetic and algebra	Geometry	Graphs	Probability

- Geometric transformations on a Cartesian plane: translation, rotation, reflection, dilatation, stretch and compression
- Transformation rule
- Equivalent figures
- Optimizing surfaces and space

PRIOR LEARNING **1** Tiling patterns

Tiling consists of covering a surface with congruent figures without any gaps and without any of the figures overlapping. Various types of congruent figures can be used to tile a surface. Below is a tiling pattern obtained by reproducing the same trapezoid:

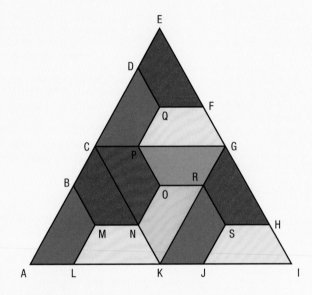

a. What type of trapezoid is reproduced in the tiling pattern?

b. What is the measure of angle:
  1) HSJ?   2) HIJ?

c. Which geometric transformation would associate polygons:
  1) LMNK and JSHI?
  2) BCNM and CPON?
  3) PGRO and GHSR?
  4) ACK and CGK?
  5) ACK and KGI?
  6) ACK and AEI?

Tiling is an ancient process that used arrangements of coloured tiles were used to decorate the walls and the floors in homes and temples.

A diamond is a mineral composed of pure carbon that has been crystallized under high pressure. Its shine and its hardness make it a very sought-after stone for jewellery and for various industrial applications.

Diamonds are cut according to shapes that allow light to reflect inside the stone and then be dispersed, giving the diamond its sparkle. The smallest stones are often cut into a shape called 8/8, composed of two regular octagonal pyramids one of which is truncated.

Three-dimensional representation of an 8/8-cut diamond

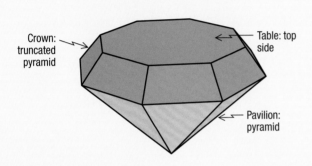

Crown: truncated pyramid

Table: top side

Pavilion: pyramid

Front view of an 8/8-cut diamond

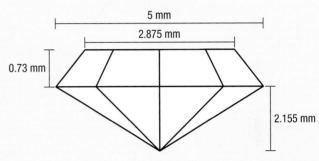

5 mm

2.875 mm

0.73 mm

2.155 mm

a. What is the perimeter of the table?

b. What is the area of the table?

c. What is the volume of the pavilion?

d. What is the volume of the crown?

> Used in relation to diamonds, the carat (symbol: ct) is a unit of mass: 5 ct = 1 g.

e. Considering that 1 cm³ of diamond has a mass of 3.52 g and a one-carat diamond has a mass of 200 mg, how many carats is this diamond?

> Diamonds are carbon crystals that were formed at elevated temperature and pressure millions of years ago in molten rock over 100 km underground.

GEOMETRIC TRANSFORMATION

A geometric transformation maps an **initial figure** onto an **image** of that figure. If a point on the initial figure is identified as A, then the corresponding point on the image of the figure is identified as A' (read "A prime").

Translation

A translation maps any initial figure onto an image of that figure based on a given **direction** and **distance**.

- The symbol *t* is used to represent a translation.
- A translation is shown by means of a translation arrow.
- The translation arrow indicates the direction and length of the translation.

E.g. Triangle A'B'C' is the image of triangle ABC under translation *t*.

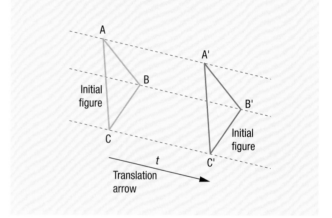

Rotation

A rotation maps any initial figure onto an image of that figure based on a given **centre, angle** and **direction** of rotation.

- The symbol *r* is used to represent a rotation.
- The centre of rotation is a fixed point.
- The angle of rotation is a measure that can be represented by a rotation arrow.
- There are two directions of rotation: clockwise and counter-clockwise. The direction can be indicated by assigning a sign to the angle of rotation. A positive sign corresponds to the counter-clockwise direction and a negative sign corresponds to the clockwise direction.

E.g. Triangle A'B'C' is the image of triangle ABC under rotation *r* with centre P and an angle of -60°.

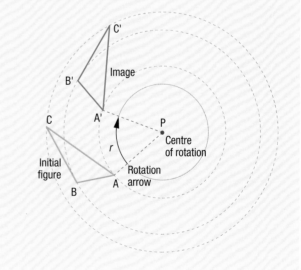

Reflection

A reflection maps any initial figure onto an image of that figure **about a line** that is provided.

- The symbol *s* is used to represent a reflection.

- The line of reflection is the straight line about which a reflection is performed.

- Any point and its image are the extremities of a segment perpendicular to the line of reflection. The line of reflection intersects this segment at its midpoint.

E.g. Triangle A'B'C' is the image of triangle ABC under reflection *s* about the given line of reflection *l*.

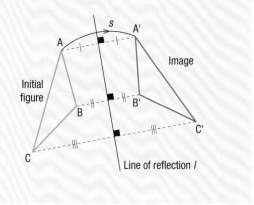

Dilatation

A dilatation maps any initial figure onto an image of that figure based on a **fixed point**, called the centre of **dilatation**, and a **factor**, called the **scale factor**.

- The symbol *h* is used to represent a dilatation.

- Under a dilatation, the image of a point is located on the straight line that passes through the initial point and the centre of dilatation.

- When point A and its image A' are both located on the same side of the centre of dilatation P, then the scale factor corresponds to:

$$\frac{\text{distance from centre of dilatation P to image point A'}}{\text{distance from centre of dilatation P to initial point A}} = \frac{m\,\overline{PA'}}{m\,\overline{PA}}$$

E.g. Triangle A'B'C' is the image of triangle ABC under dilatation *h* with centre P and scale factor 0.5.

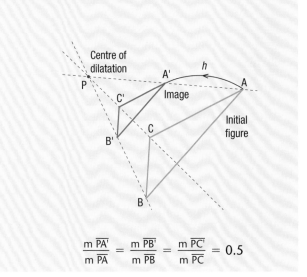

$$\frac{m\,\overline{PA'}}{m\,\overline{PA}} = \frac{m\,\overline{PB'}}{m\,\overline{PB}} = \frac{m\,\overline{PC'}}{m\,\overline{PC}} = 0.5$$

AREA OF A FIGURE

Figure			
Figure			
Area	$A_{triangle} = \dfrac{b \times h}{2}$	$A_{trapezoid} = \dfrac{(B + b) \times h}{2}$	$A_{parallelogram} = b \times h$
Figure			
Area	$A_{rhombus} = \dfrac{D \times d}{2}$	$A_{rectangle} = b \times h$	$A_{square} = s^2$
Figure			
Area	$A_{regular\ polygon} = \dfrac{perimeter \times apothem}{2}$	$A_{circle} = \pi r^2$	$A_{sphere} = 4\pi r^2$

VOLUME OF A SOLID

Solid	Volume
• Right prism • Right-circular cylinder	$V = (\text{area of the base}) \times (\text{height})$
• Right pyramid • Right-circular cone	$V = \dfrac{(\text{area of the base}) \times (\text{height})}{3}$
• Sphere	$V = \dfrac{4\pi r^3}{3}$

knowledge in action

1 For each case, indicate which geometric transformation maps the initial figure onto its image.

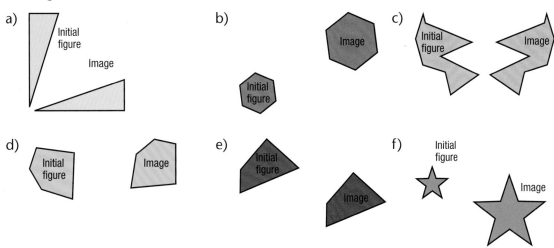

a)   Initial figure   Image

b)   Image   Initial figure

c)   Initial figure   Image

d)   Initial figure   Image

e)   Initial figure   Image

f)   Initial figure   Image

2 Calculate the area of each of the following figures.

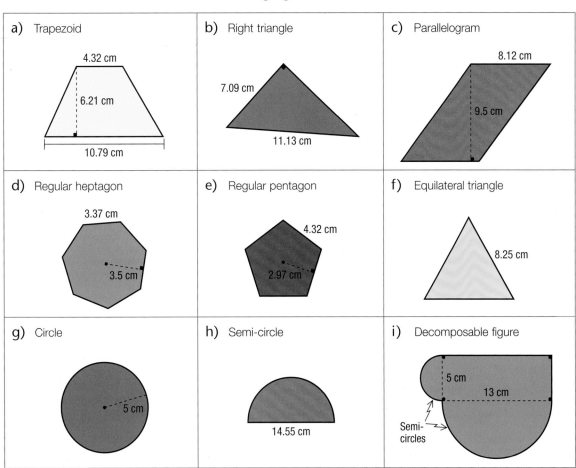

a) Trapezoid
  4.32 cm
  6.21 cm
  10.79 cm

b) Right triangle
  7.09 cm
  11.13 cm

c) Parallelogram
  8.12 cm
  9.5 cm

d) Regular heptagon
  3.37 cm
  3.5 cm

e) Regular pentagon
  4.32 cm
  2.97 cm

f) Equilateral triangle
  8.25 cm

g) Circle
  5 cm

h) Semi-circle
  14.55 cm

i) Decomposable figure
  5 cm
  13 cm
  Semi-circles

3 For each case, find the centre of dilatation that associates the two figures.

a)

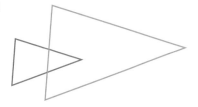

b)

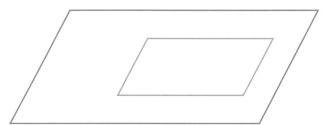

c)

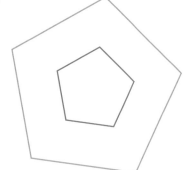

d)

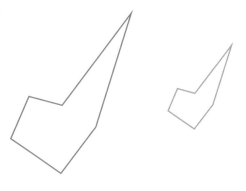

4 Calculate the volume of each of the following solids.

a) Regular square-based prism	b) Regular square-based pyramid	c) Sphere
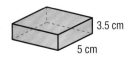 3.5 cm 5 cm	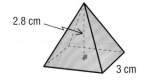 2.8 cm 3 cm	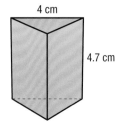 5 cm
d) Regular tetrahedron	**e)** Regular triangular-based prism	**f)** Right-circular cone
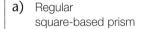 7.5 cm	4 cm 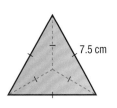 4.7 cm	 28.3 cm 2.4 cm
g) Right trapezoidal-based prism	**h)** Right-circular cylinder	**i)** Decomposable solid
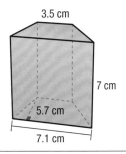 3.5 cm 7 cm 5.7 cm 7.1 cm	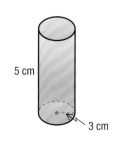 5 cm 3 cm	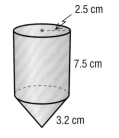 2.5 cm 7.5 cm 3.2 cm

5 Observe the two adjacent right rectangular-based prisms. Prism Ⓑ is an enlargement of Prism Ⓐ.

What is the ratio of:

a) similarity?

b) their areas?

c) their volumes?

Prism Ⓐ

Prism Ⓑ

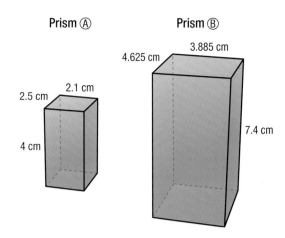

6 **CYLINDRO-CONICAL** Various sectors of the construction industry use cylindro-conical containers composed of a right-circular cylinder placed over a right-circular cone. The surface area of a cylindro-conical container is 88.6 m². What is the surface area of a similar cylindro-conical container whose capacity:

a) is double?

b) is 50% greater?

c) is half?

A cylindro-conical silo for cement storage

7 A regular triangular-based prism is inscribed in a right-circular cylinder with a radius of 4 cm and a height of 7 cm.

a) What is the surface area of:
   1) the cylinder?   2) the prism?

b) What is the volume of:
   1) the cylinder?   2) the prism?

8 For each case, identify a geometric transformation that associates two congruent parts of the illustrated object.

a)

b)

c)

9 In order to depict a solid using central projection with one vanishing point, a dilatation with centre P and scale factor 0.75 is applied to regular hexagon ABCDEF. If the perimeter of hexagon ABCDEF is 12 cm and if m $\overline{AP}$ = 24 cm, determine the volume of the regular prism shown below.

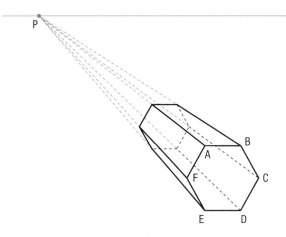

10 By connecting the midpoints of 8 edges of a cube, another prism is created.

a) What type of prism is this?

b) What percentage of the original cube's volume does the new prism's volume represent?

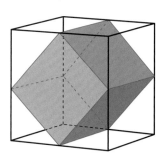

11 a) The adjacent sphere has a radius of 250 cm.

Calculate:

1) its area　　　　2) its volume

b) The sphere is cut into two hemispheres.
Calculate the sum of:

1) their areas　　　　2) their volumes

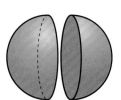

c) Each hemisphere is cut into quarter-spheres.
Calculate the sum of:

1) their areas　　　　2) their volumes

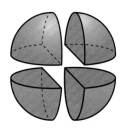

12 The tiling pattern below is comprised of small equilateral triangles, each with an area of 8.17 cm². What is the length of segment AB?

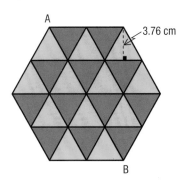

A

3.76 cm

B

13 The two circular cylinders below have the same radius and the same height.

a) Do they have the same area? Explain your answer.

b) Do they have the same volume? Explain your answer.

14 Equilateral triangles ABC and A'B'C' are associated by a dilatation. For each case, find the scale factor.

a) A side of triangle ABC measures 7.28 cm and its corresponding side of triangle A'B'C' measures 18.2 cm.

b) A side of triangle ABC measures 9.39 cm and the perimeter of triangle A'B'C' is 23.48 cm.

c) The perimeter of triangle ABC is 1.86 cm and the perimeter of triangle A'B'C' is 9.29 cm.

d) The area of triangle ABC is 11.2 cm² and the area of triangle A'B'C' is 70 cm².

e) The perimeter of triangle ABC is 6.78 cm and the area of triangle A'B'C' is 58.61 cm².

 15 A poster advertising a fireworks competition contains seven stars. Each red star is associated with the yellow star by completing a different dilatation. Using the sheet provided, draw the convex polygon obtained by connecting the centres of all the dilatations.

The colour of fireworks depends on the materials used. For example, copper will produce blue and barium green. Aluminium is used to create sparks, and zinc is used to create smoke.

This section is related to LES 4.

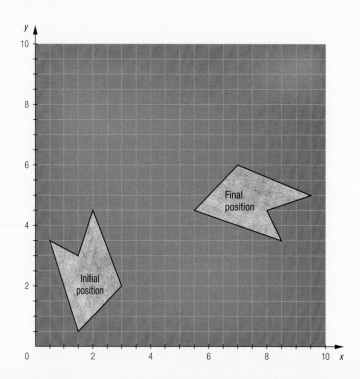

PROBLEM Gone with the wind!

When a violent gust of wind occurs, many objects can be flipped upside down, blown away and damaged.

On a construction site, a sheet of plywood that had been placed on the ground was displaced by a gust of wind. The illustration below shows its initial position and its final position.

Using geometric transformations, describe how it would be possible to associate the initial position of the sheet of plywood with its final position.

In the Wreckhouse region of southwestern Newfoundland and Labrador, the wind regularly blows at speeds that can reach 150 km/h, which is equivalent to a Category 2 hurricane.

Artistic geometry

Maurits Cornelis Escher (1898-1972) dedicated his life to etching and graphic arts. In addition to his great love of architecture and the arts, Escher often used geometric transformations as inspiration for his works.

Below, a Cartesian plane has been superimposed onto an Escher print, entitled *Eight Heads*, which the artist created in 1922. The origin of the plane is the centre of the print. One of the features of this work is that each of the elements can be mapped onto another identical element by a translation.

a. Calculate the difference:

 1) (x-coordinate of point A') – (x-coordinate of point A)

 2) (y-coordinate of point A') – (y-coordinate of point A)

 3) (x-coordinate of point B') – (x-coordinate of point B)

 4) (y-coordinate of point B') – (y-coordinate of point B)

b. Compare the results obtained in a.

c. Find the coordinates:

 1) of point C'

 2) of point D

Below, a Cartesian plane has been superimposed onto an Escher print. The origin of the plane is the centre of the print. Each of the work's elements can be mapped onto another identical element by a clockwise rotation of 90° about the origin.

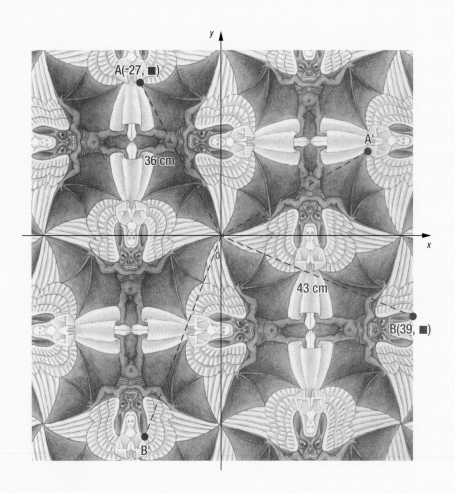

d. What are the coordinates of:
  1) point A?
  2) point A'?

e. Compare the coordinates obtained in question d.

f. What are the coordinates of:
  1) point B?
  2) point B'?

g. Compare the coordinates obtained in question f.

h. What conjecture can you formulate regarding the coordinates of two points that are associated by a rotation of -90° about the origin on a Cartesian plane?

i. Determine two other angles of rotations about the origin that would map an element of the print onto another identical element.

Below, a Cartesian plane has been superimposed onto an Escher print. The *x*-coordinates correspond to the horizontal position (in cm), and the *y*-coordinates correspond to the vertical position (in cm) with respect to the centre of the print. Each of the work's elements can be mapped onto another identical element by a reflection about the *y*-axis.

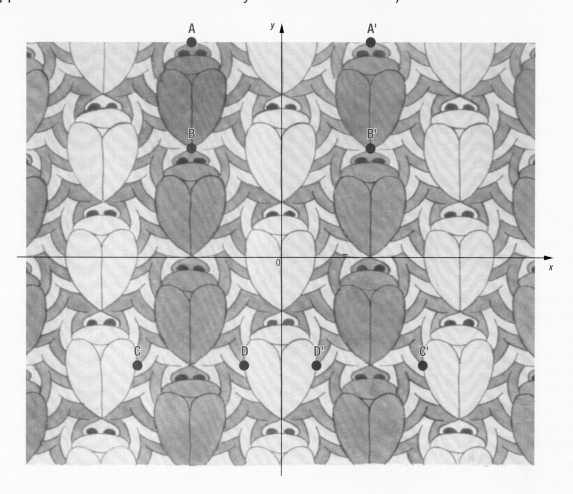

Below are the dimensions of each of the scarabs that make up the print:

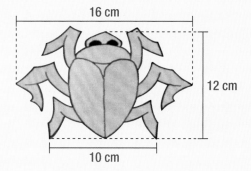

j. Determine the coordinates of the following points.

  1) A and A'   2) B and B'   3) C and C'   4) D and D'

k. Compare each of the coordinates obtained in **j**.

l. What conjecture can you formulate regarding the coordinates of two points associated by a reflection about the *y*-axis?

Techno math

Dynamic geometry software allows you to draw figures on a Cartesian plane and apply various geometric transformations. By using the tools SHOW THE AXES, GRID, TRIANGLE and COORDINATES tools, you are able to:

- define a translation with the VECTOR and TRANSLATION tools
- define a rotation with the NUMBER and ROTATION tools
- define a reflection with the AXIAL SYMMETRY tool

a. Refer to Screen **1** and answer the following:

1) Which of the two figures corresponds to the initial figure? Explain your answer.

2) Find the rule that allows you to determine the coordinates of the vertices of the image based on the coordinates of the vertices of the initial triangle.

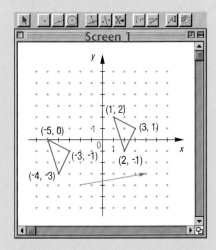

b. Refer to Screen **2** and answer the following:

1) Where is the centre of rotation located?

2) Which of the two figures corresponds to the image? Explain your answer.

3) Find the rule that allows you to determine the coordinates of the vertices of the image based on the coordinates of the vertices of the initial triangle.

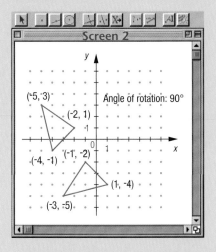

c. Refer to Screen **3** and answer the following:

1) Where is the line of reflection located?

2) Find the rule that allows you to determine the coordinates of the vertices of the image based on the coordinates of the vertices of the initial triangle.

d. Using dynamic geometry software, explore different cases in order to find the rule that allows you to find the coordinates of the vertices of the image of a triangle based on the coordinates of the vertices of an initial triangle for CENTRAL SYMMETRY with respect to the origin of the Cartesian plane.

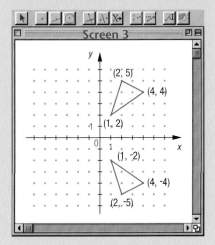

GEOMETRIC TRANSFORMATIONS IN THE CARTESIAN PLANE

Performing a geometric transformation in a Cartesian plane consists of mapping points on the plane onto other points on the same plane.

Geometric transformations that associate congruent figures are **isometries**. **Translations, rotations** and **reflections** are isometries.

Translation

In a Cartesian plane, a translation t of a units parallel to the x-axis and b units parallel to the y-axis can be defined according to the following rule.

$$t_{(a, b)}: (x, y) \mapsto (x + a, y + b)$$

E.g.

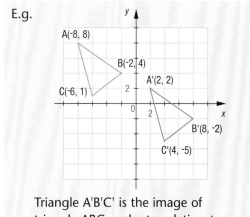

Triangle A'B'C' is the image of triangle ABC under translation $t_{(10, -6)}$.

Rotation

In a Cartesian plane, a rotation r about the origin O with an angle of rotation that is a multiple of 90° clockwise or counter-clockwise can be defined according to a rule.

- A rotation of -90° or 270° about the origin can be defined according to the following rule.

- A rotation of -180° or 180° about the origin can be defined according to the following rule.

$$r_{(O, -90°)} \text{ or } r_{(O, 270°)}: (x, y) \mapsto (y, -x)$$

$$r_{(O, -180°)} \text{ or } r_{(O, 180°)}: (x, y) \mapsto (-x, -y)$$

E.g.

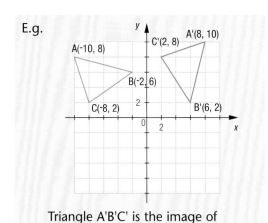

Triangle A'B'C' is the image of triangle ABC under rotation $r_{(O, -90°)}$.

E.g.

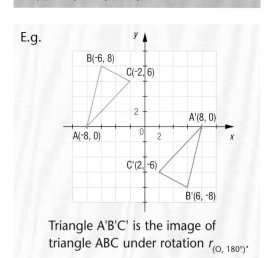

Triangle A'B'C' is the image of triangle ABC under rotation $r_{(O, 180°)}$.

- A rotation of 90° or -270° about the origin can be defined according to the following rule.

$$r_{(O, 90°)} \text{ or } r_{(O, -270°)}:$$
$$(x, y) \mapsto (-y, x)$$

E.g.

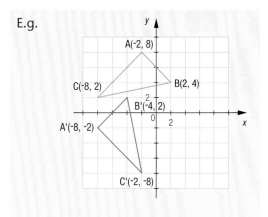

Triangle A'B'C' is the image of triangle ABC under rotation $r_{(O, 90°)}$.

Reflection

In a Cartesian plane, a reflection s about one of the axes can be defined according to a rule.

- A reflection about the x-axis can be defined according to the following rule.

$$s_x: (x, y) \mapsto (x, -y)$$

E.g.

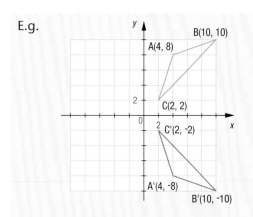

Triangle A'B'C' is the image of triangle ABC under reflection s_x.

- A reflection about the y-axis can be defined according to the following rule.

$$s_y: (x, y) \mapsto (-x, y)$$

E.g.

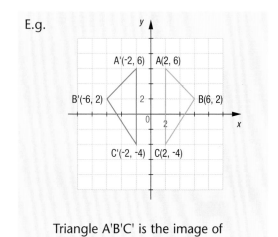

Triangle A'B'C' is the image of triangle ABC under reflection s_y.

practice 2.1

1 Complete the tables below.

a)

Initial point	Image under translation $t_{(3, -5)}$
A(4, 0)	A'(,)
B(-9, 4)	B'(,)
C(12, -33)	C'(,)
D(-7, -5)	D'(,)

b)

Initial point	Image under rotation $r_{(O, 90°)}$
E(5, 8)	E'(,)
F(-7, 0)	F'(,)
G(10, -5)	G'(,)
H(-2, -9)	H'(,)

c)

Initial point	Image under reflection s_x
I(18, 69)	I'(,)
J(-99, 24)	J'(,)
K(57, 0)	K'(,)
L(-88, -12)	L'(,)

2 For each of the graphical representations below, do the following:

1) Find the transformation rule that associates the two figures.
2) Determine the coordinates of the vertices that are missing.

a)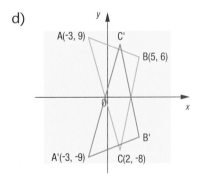

b)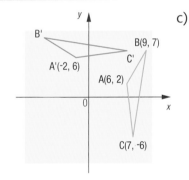

c)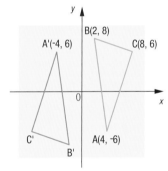

d)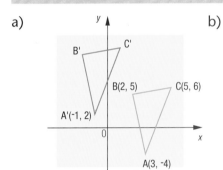

e)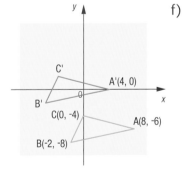

f)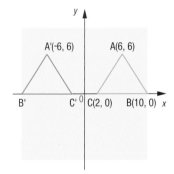

g)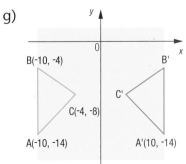

h)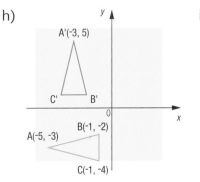

i)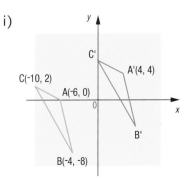

3 For each case, find the rule for the transformation that associates the two points.

a) the translation that associates A(3, 8) and A'(9, -2)

b) the rotation that associates B(2, -6) and B'(-2, 6)

c) the reflection that associates C(3, -8) and C'(-3, -8)

d) the reflection that associates D(1, 9) and D'(1, -9)

e) the rotation that associates E(12, 17) and E'(-17, 12)

4 Complete the tables below.

a)

Initial point	Image
(3, -5)	(5, 3)
(6, 2)	(-2, 6)
(9, -1)	(1, 9)
(7, -5)	
(3, 3)	
(12, 7)	
(x, y)	

b)

Initial point	Image
(8, 17)	(-8, 17)
(3, -5)	(-3, -5)
(4, 5)	(-4, 5)
(-1, -1)	
(5, -4)	
(7, -5)	
(x, y)	

c)

Initial point	Image
(1, -6)	(-1, 6)
(7, -5)	(-7, 5)
(5, -4)	(-5, 4)
(8, 4)	
(4, 5)	
(-2, -5)	
(x, y)	

5 Draw the image of the figure resulting from the indicated translation.

a)

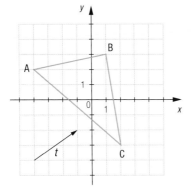

b)

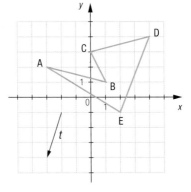

c) translation $t_{(4, -2)}$

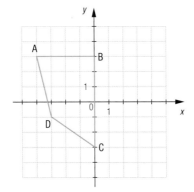

d) translation $t_{(-3, -3)}$

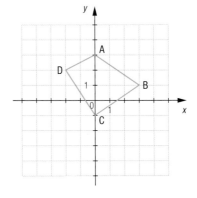

6 Draw the image of the figure resulting from the indicated rotation.

a) rotation $r_{(O, 90°)}$

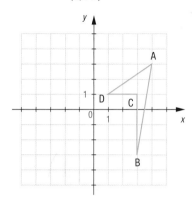

b) rotation $r_{(O, -90°)}$

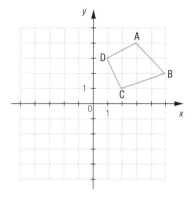

c) rotation $r_{(O, 180°)}$

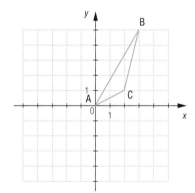

d) rotation $r_{(O, 270°)}$

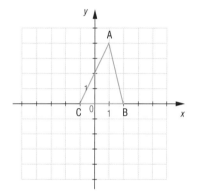

7 The two graphs below respectively represent a reflection about the bisector of the 1st and 3rd quadrants and a reflection about the bisector of the 2nd and 4th quadrants.

Graph ①

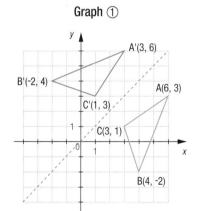

Graph ②

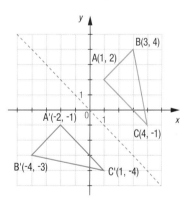

a) Which of the graphs shown above has a line of reflection whose equation is:

1) $y = x$?   2) $y = -x$?

b) What conjecture can you formulate regarding the transformation rule:

1) of a reflection about the bisector of the 1st and 3rd quadrants?

2) of a reflection about the bisector of the 2nd and 4th quadrants?

8 For each of the graphs below, do the following:

1) Indicate whether the figures are associated by a translation, rotation or reflection.
2) Determine the transformation rule that associates the two figures.

a)
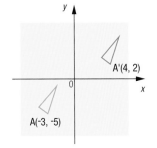

b)
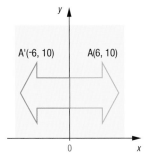

c)
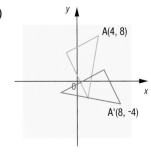

d)
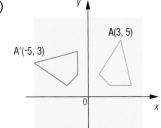

e)
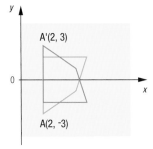

f)
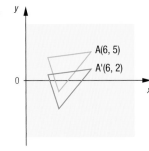

g)
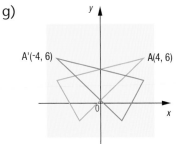

h)
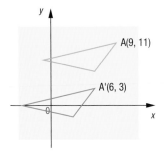

i)
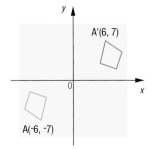

9 For each of the tables below, do the following:

1) Draw the initial figure and its image in a Cartesian plane.
2) Determine the transformation rule that associates the two figures.

a)

Initial vertex	Image
A(3, 8)	A'(7, 8)
B(6, -9)	B'(10, -9)
C(5, 1)	C'(9, 1)

b)

Initial vertex	Image
A(5, 25)	A'(-25, 5)
B(2, -2)	B'(2, 2)
C(8, 8)	C'(-8, 8)

c)

Initial vertex	Image
A(21, 7)	A'(21, -7)
B(3, 1)	B'(3, -1)
C(3, -4)	C'(3, 4)

d)

Initial vertex	Image
A(8, 0)	A'(8, 0)
B(6, -5)	B'(6, 5)
C(2, 3)	C'(2, -3)

e)

Initial vertex	Image
A(9, -9)	A'(9, 9)
B(5, 4)	B'(-4, 5)
C(8, 1)	C'(-1, 8)

f)

Initial vertex	Image
A(2, 2)	A'(-3, 5)
B(3, 4)	B'(-2, 7)
C(19, 5)	C'(14, 8)

10 For each of the geometric transformations described below, complete the table.

	Transformation rule	Description	Initial figure and image
a)		Add 10 units to the *x*-coordinate and subtract 8 units from the *y*-coordinate.	A'(6, -6)
b)		A clockwise rotation of 90° about the origin.	B(4, 8)
c)			C(21, 9) C'(21, -9)
d)			D(1, 8) D'(-1, -8)

11 Following are the rules for two exponential functions: $f(x) = 2^x$ and $g(x) = \left(\frac{1}{2}\right)^x$.

a) Complete the adjacent tables of values.

b) What do you notice when you compare the ordered pairs in the tables of values for functions f and g?

c) On the same Cartesian plane, draw the curves associated with functions f and g.

d) What geometric transformation associates the curves of these two functions?

x	f(x)
-3	■
-2	■
-1	■
0	■
1	■
2	■
3	■

x	g(x)
-3	■
-2	■
-1	■
0	■
1	■
2	■
3	■

12 For each case, what geometric transformation directly associates triangles ABC and A"B"C"?

a) Graph ① shows the image of triangle ABC under reflection s_y as well as the image of triangle A'B'C' under reflection s_x.

Graph ①

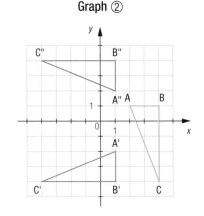

b) Graph ② shows the image of triangle ABC under rotation $r_{(O, -90°)}$, as well as the image of triangle A'B'C' under reflection s_x.

Graph ②

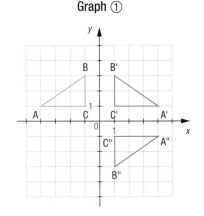

13 The coordinates of point A are (3, 16).

a) If you apply translation $t_{(6, 10)}$, then rotation $r_{(O, 90°)}$ and finally reflection s_x to the Cartesian plane, what is the image of point A?

b) If you apply rotation $r_{(O, 90°)}$, then translation $t_{(6, 10)}$ and finally reflection s_x to the Cartesian plane, what is the image of point A?

c) 1) Compare the results obtained in questions **a)** and **b)**.

 2) What conjecture can you formulate regarding the coordinates of an image of a point based on the order in which a series of geometric transformations is performed?

SECTION 2.2 — Dilatation, stretch and compression in the Cartesian plane

This section is related to LES 4.

PROBLEM   Distortion

Images observed in a mirror that has one or more curves are distorted from reality. Depending on the size, number and position of the curves, the distortions will be more or less emphasized and the effects will vary.

Images can also be distorted using drawing software. The following is an example:

Distortion generated by software

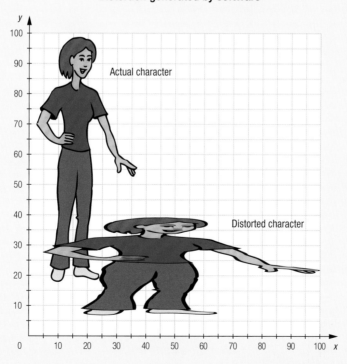

Actual character

Distorted character

Describe a transformation rule that would map the actual character onto the distorted character.

ACTIVITY 1 A multiplicative transformation

One of the geometric transformations that can be applied to a Cartesian plane is obtained by multiplying the coordinates of each point on the plane by the same number.

a. Referring to the adjacent figures, multiply the coordinates of the vertices:

1) of triangle ABC by 1.5, and draw the resulting triangle A'B'C'

2) of triangle DEF by 0.5, and draw the resulting triangle D'E'F'

3) of triangle GHI by -2, and draw the resulting triangle G'H'I'

b. For each case, do the following:

1) Decide if the image obtained is congruent to the initial figure. Explain your answer.

2) Decide if the image obtained is similar to the initial figure. Explain your answer.

3) Compare the slope of the corresponding sides. What do you notice?

4) What is the name of the geometric transformation that associates the two figures?

5) Draw three straight lines, each passing through corresponding vertices. What does the intersection of these three straight lines correspond to?

6) What is the ratio $\dfrac{\text{perimeter of the image}}{\text{perimeter of the initial figure}}$?

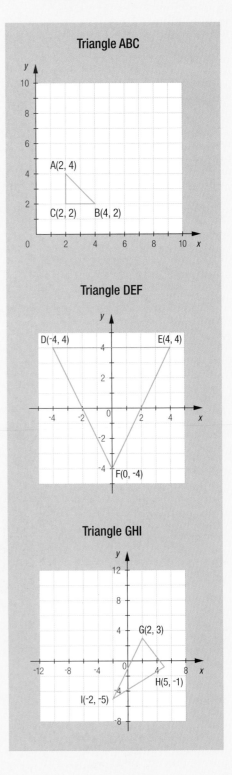

Triangle ABC

Triangle DEF

Triangle GHI

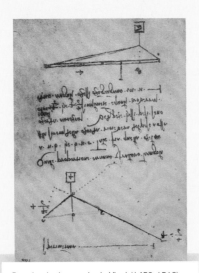

The triangle is one of the geometric figure that has been the most studied over the centuries.

Drawing by Leonardo da Vinci (1452-1519) that illustrates the proportions of a triangle.

Another geometric transformation that can be applied to a Cartesian plane is obtained by multiplying either the *x*-coordinate or the *y*-coordinate of each point on the plane by the same number.

c. Referring to the adjacent figures, do the following:

1) Multiply the *x*-coordinates of the points of quadrilateral JKLM by 2, and draw the resulting quadrilateral J'K'L'M'.

2) Multiply the *y*-coordinates of the points of quadrilateral NOPQ by 0.5, and draw the resulting quadrilateral N'O'P'Q'.

3) Multiply the *x*-coordinates of the points of quadrilateral RSTU by -0.5 and the *y*-coordinates by 3, and draw the resulting quadrilateral R'S'T'U'.

d. For each case, do the following:

1) Compare the shape of the initial figure to the shape of the image. What do you notice?

2) Decide if the image obtained is congruent to the initial figure. Explain your answer.

3) Decide if the image obtained is similar to the initial figure. Explain your answer.

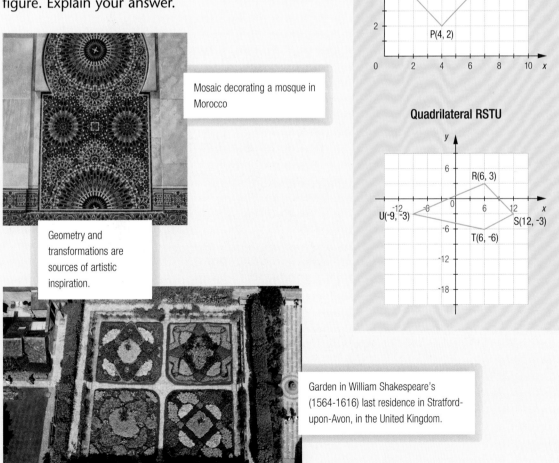

Quadrilateral JKLM

Quadrilateral NOPQ

Quadrilateral RSTU

Mosaic decorating a mosque in Morocco

Geometry and transformations are sources of artistic inspiration.

Garden in William Shakespeare's (1564-1616) last residence in Stratford-upon-Avon, in the United Kingdom.

Techno math

Dynamic geometry software allows you to draw figures in the Cartesian plane and apply various geometric transformations to them. By using the tools SHOW THE AXES, GRID, TRIANGLE, NUMBER, COORDINATES and DILATATION tools, you can define a dilatation in the Cartesian plane.

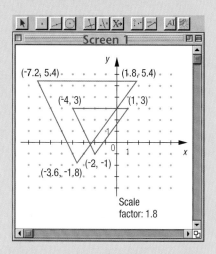

a. For each of the adjacent screens, do the following:

    1) Determine which of the two figures is the initial figure.

    2) Identify the centre of dilatation.

    3) Find the rule that allows you to determine the coordinates of the vertices of the image based on the coordinates of the vertices of the initial triangle.

b. Which of the adjacent screens contains two figures with different orientations?

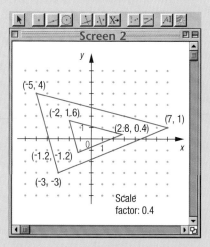

c. 1) Using dynamic geometry software, explore different cases in order to find the rule that allows you to determine the coordinates of the vertices of an image based on the coordinates of the vertices of an initial triangle for a dilatation whose centre is the origin of the Cartesian plane.

    2) Using dynamic geometry software, explore the transformation called CENTRAL SYMMETRY by using the origin of the Cartesian plane as the centre.

    3) Under what conditions can a dilatation correspond to a central symmetry?

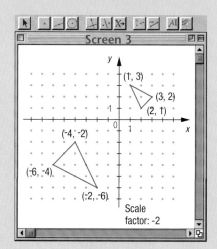

CHANGE OF SCALE

In a Cartesian plane, a change of scale is a transformation defined by the rule $(x, y) \mapsto (ax, by)$ where **a** and **b** are non-zero constant numbers. Depending on the values of **a** and **b**, a change of scale can correspond to a dilatation, a stretch or a compression.

Dilatation

In a Cartesian plane, a dilatation h whose centre O corresponds to the origin of the plane and whose scale factor **a** is non-zero can be defined according to the following rule.

$$h_{(O,\,a)}: (x, y) \mapsto (ax, ay)$$

- If $0 < |a| < 1$, the image is a **reduction** of the initial figure.

- If $|a| = 1$, the image is **congruent** to the initial figure.

- If $|a| > 1$, the image is an **enlargement** of the initial figure.

- If $a > 0$, the initial figure and its image are located on **the same side** of the centre of dilatation.

- If $a < 0$, the initial figure and its image are located on **opposite sides** of the centre of dilatation.

E.g. 1) Triangle A'B'C' is the image of triangle ABC under dilatation $h_{(O,\,3)}$.

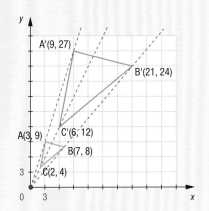

The image triangle is an enlargement of the original triangle.

2) Triangle A'B'C' is the image of triangle ABC under dilatation $h_{(O,\,-\frac{2}{3})}$.

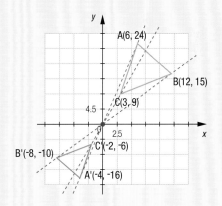

The image triangle is a reduction of the original triangle.

Stretch and compression

Multiplying the x-coordinates of the Cartesian plane by the constant **a** produces a horizontal scale change. More precisely, it causes a horizontal stretch (if $|a| > 1$) or a horizontal compression (if $0 < |a| < 1$), in addition to a reflection about the y-axis (if $a < 0$). A horizontal scale change can be defined according to the following rule.

Horizontal scale change: $(x, y) \mapsto (ax, y)$

E.g. 1) Triangle A'B'C' is the image of triangle ABC under horizontal scale change $(x, y) \mapsto (3x, y)$.

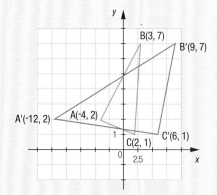

The image triangle is a horizontal stretch of the initial triangle.

2) Triangle A'B'C' is the image of triangle ABC under horizontal scale change $(x, y) \mapsto (0.5x, y)$.

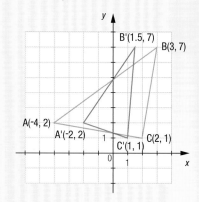

The image triangle is a horizontal compression of the initial triangle.

Multiplying the y-coordinates of the Cartesian plane by the constant **b** produces a vertical scale change. More precisely, it causes a vertical stretch (if $|b| > 1$) or a vertical compression (if $0 < |b| < 1$), in addition to a reflection about the x-axis (if $b < 0$). A vertical scale change can be defined according to the following rule.

> Vertical scale change: $(x, y) \mapsto (x, by)$

E.g. 1) Triangle A'B'C' is the image of triangle ABC under vertical scale change $(x, y) \mapsto (x, 2y)$.

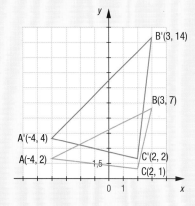

The image triangle is a vertical stretch of the initial triangle.

2) Triangle A'B'C' is the image of triangle ABC under vertical scale change $(x, y) \mapsto (x, -0.25y)$.

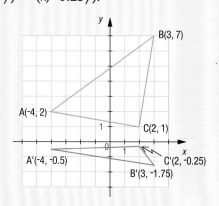

The image triangle is a vertical compression of the initial triangle.

practice 2.2

1 For each of the graphs below, do the following:

1) Indicate whether the figures are associated by a dilatation, horizontal stretch, vertical stretch, horizontal compression or vertical compression.

2) Determine the transformation rule that associates these two figures.

a)
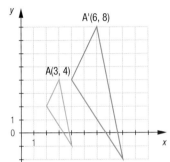

b)
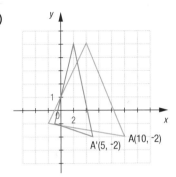

c)
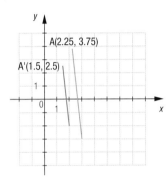

d)
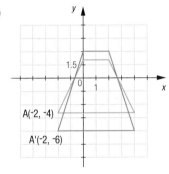

e)
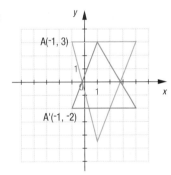

f)
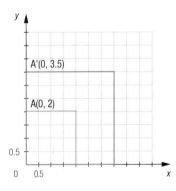

g)
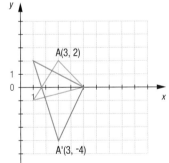

h)
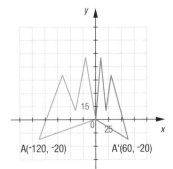

i)
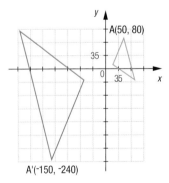

2 For each ordered pair, find the rule for the scale change that generates the coordinates of the image.

a) A(2, 7) and A'(6, 21)

b) B(8, -10) and B'(4, -10)

c) C(5, -7) and C'(5, 21)

d) D(2, 2) and D'(-4, -4)

e) E(8, -8) and E'(8, 2)

f) F(2, 7) and F'(-4, -14)

3 Draw the image of each of the following figures based on the transformation rule provided.

a) $(x, y) \mapsto (2x, 2y)$

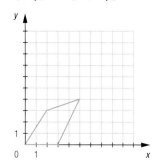

b) $(x, y) \mapsto (1.5x, 1.5y)$

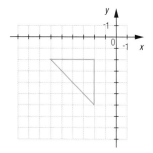

c) $(x, y) \mapsto (-2x, -2y)$

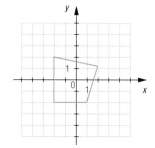

d) $(x, y) \mapsto (x, 2y)$

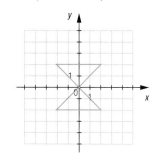

e) $(x, y) \mapsto (2x, y)$

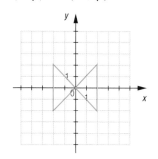

f) $(x, y) \mapsto (-x, y)$

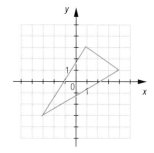

g) $(x, y) \mapsto (x, -0.5y)$

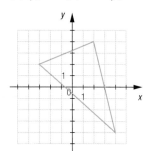

h) $(x, y) \mapsto (-0.5x, y)$

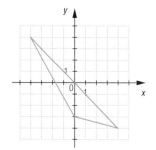

i) $(x, y) \mapsto (x, -y)$

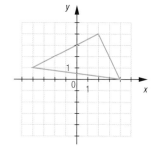

4 For each of the tables below, do the following:

1) Draw the initial triangle and its image on a Cartesian plane.
2) Provide the transformation rule that associates the two triangles.

a)

Initial vertex	Image
A(2, -7)	A'(-6, 21)
B(5, 15)	B'(-15, -45)
C(3, 4)	C'(-9, -12)

b)

Initial vertex	Image
A(4, 8)	A'(16, 8)
B(9, -1)	B'(36, -1)
C(5, 7)	C'(20, 7)

c)

Initial vertex	Image
A(5, 3)	A'(2.5, 1.5)
B(2, 1)	B'(1, 0.5)
C(-4, 8)	C'(-2, 4)

d)

Initial vertex	Image
A(3, 8)	A'(3, 2)
B(6, 21)	B'(6, 5.25)
C(5, 4)	C'(5, 1)

e)

Initial vertex	Image
A(5, 25)	A'(25, 125)
B(26, 13)	B'(130, 65)
C(4, 9)	C'(20, 45)

f)

Initial vertex	Image
A(8, 16)	A'(16, 16)
B(5, 3)	B'(10, 3)
C(7, -9)	C'(14, -9)

5 For each of the graphs below, do the following:

1) Provide the transformation rule that associates the two figures.
2) Determine the coordinates of the vertices B' and C'.

a)
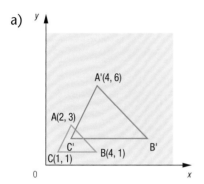

b)
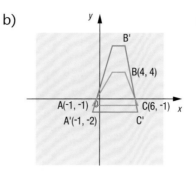

c)
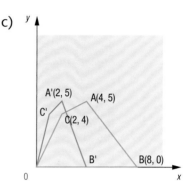

d)
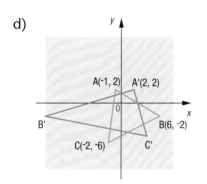

e)
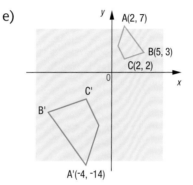

f)
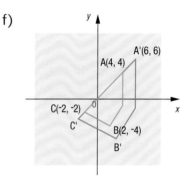

6 Each of the graphs below displays curves associated by a vertical stretch or vertical compression.

First-degree polynomial functions
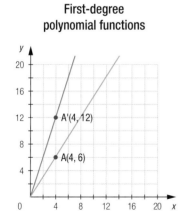

Second-degree polynomial functions
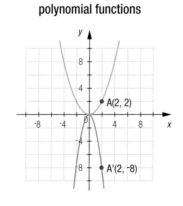

Exponential functions
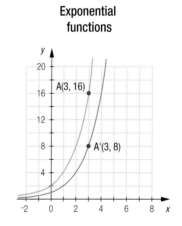

a) For each of the graphs, do the following:

1) Determine the rule of each function.
2) Determine the transformation rule that associates the two curves.

b) What link can you establish between the answers obtained in **a) 1)** and those obtained in **a) 2)**?

7 Photograph ② below is a distortion of Photograph ①.

Photograph ①

12.7 cm

10 cm

Photograph ②

12.7 cm

12.7 cm

Describe the transformations that must be performed on Photograph ② in order to obtain a photograph whose dimensions are 15% larger than those of Photograph ①.

8 Identify two successive geometric transformations that would associate quadrilaterals ABCD and A'B'C'D'.

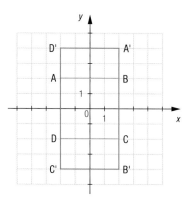

9 Find the rule of a geometric transformation that would associate the two circles below.

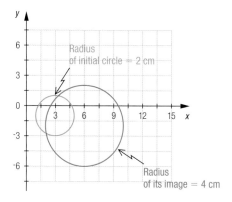

10 Each of the graphs below shows figures associated by a dilatation centred at the origin. For each case, determine the scale factor.

a)

b)

c)

d)

11 What other geometric transformation is equivalent to a dilatation centred at the origin with a scale factor of ⁻1?

12 **SOUND WAVES** An oscilloscope is a device that measures sound waves and represents them with curves. The adjacent graph displays a representation of three sound waves obtained by varying the sound's volume, otherwise known as its amplitude.

a) What are the y-intercepts of the three curves?

b) What type of scale change can be applied to Curve ❶ to obtain:

   1) Curve ❷?

   2) Curve ❸?

c) Determine the transformation rule that allows you to obtain Curve ❸ from:

   1) Curve ❶

   2) Curve ❷

Oscilloscope displaying three sound waves

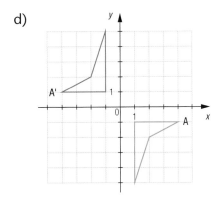

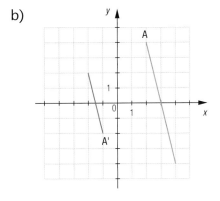

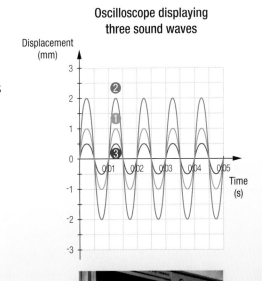

An oscilloscope is used to visualize electric voltage.

13 Each of the following graphs contains three snowflake models associated by dilatations centred at the origin. For each case, determine the scale factor that transforms the blue snowflake into the yellow snowflake.

a) Transformation that associates the blue snowflake with the pink snowflake is $h_{(O, 2)}$.

Transformation that associates the pink snowflake with the yellow snowflake is $h_{(O, 2)}$.

b) Transformation that associates the blue snowflake with the pink snowflake is $h_{(O, 4)}$.

Transformation that associates the pink snowflake with the yellow snowflake is $h_{(O, 2)}$.

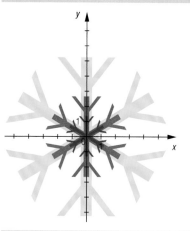

c) Transformation that associates the blue snowflake with the pink snowflake is $h_{\left(O, -\frac{1}{3}\right)}$.

Transformation that associates the pink snowflake with the yellow snowflake is $h_{(O, -4)}$.

d) Transformation that associates the blue snowflake with the pink snowflake is $h_{(O, -2)}$.

Transformation that associates the pink snowflake with the yellow snowflake is $h_{(O, 0.75)}$.

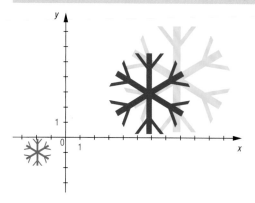

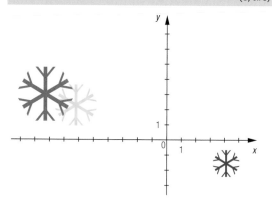

A snow crystal's shape depends on the air temperature when it is formed in the clouds. For example, when the air temperature is between 0°C and -4°C, snowflakes are thin, flat and hexagonal. Between -4°C and -6°C, their branches take the shape of needles. Between -10°C and -12°C, snowflakes have six long points.

SECTION 2.3 Equivalent figures

This section is related to LES 5 and 6.

 PROBLEM Painting

Patrick has to paint the concrete basement floor of two community centres. He must anticipate the amount of paint needed to complete this task. One litre of paint covers 9 m² of concrete.

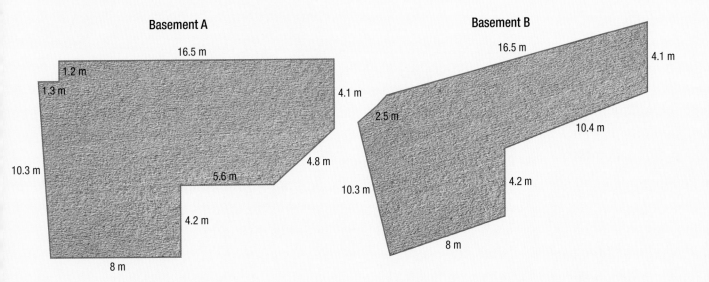

Basement A

16.5 m
1.2 m
1.3 m
10.3 m
5.6 m
4.8 m
4.2 m
8 m

Basement B

16.5 m
4.1 m
2.5 m
4.1 m
10.4 m
4.2 m
10.3 m
8 m

In order to calculate the area of the basement, Patrick first measures its perimeter. To determine the area, he then calculates the area of a square that has the same perimeter.

 What do you think of Patrick's method?

Pigments give liquids their colour. Known since antiquity, these substances originally came from a variety of natural sources, including plants. For example, indigo came from the indigo plant and saffron from the style of crocus-saffron plant, the most expensive food substance in the world. Other pigments such as purple came from the shells of the Murex snail and carmine from the cochineal insect. Others, such as ochre, originated in minerals. Today, most pigments are synthetic.

The two plots of land below must be fenced in and covered with grass.

Plot A

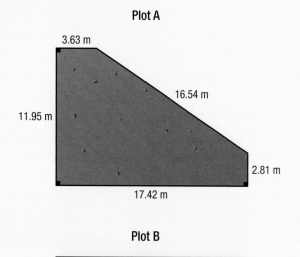

3.63 m

16.54 m

11.95 m

2.81 m

17.42 m

Plot B

6.175 m

20 m

Artificial grass can be installed on many types of surfaces. There are many advantages: no watering, no fertilizing, no cutting, it remains green year-round and it can be custom-made for sports terrains.

a. Compare:

1) the shape of the plots

2) the perimeter of the plots

3) the area of the plots

b. Of the two plots, which one will:

1) cost more to enclose with a fence?

2) cost less to cover with grass?

c. Do two plots of land with the same shape necessarily have:

1) the same perimeter? Explain your answer.

2) the same area? Explain your answer.

d. Do two plots of land with the same perimeter necessarily have:

1) the same shape? Explain your answer.

2) the same area? Explain your answer.

e. Do two plots of land with the same area necessarily have:

1) the same shape? Explain your answer.

2) the same perimeter? Explain your answer.

f. Of the statements below, which describe two identical plots of land?

A Two plots of land with the same shape and the same perimeter.

B Two plots of land with the same shape and the same area.

C Two plots of land with the same perimeter and the same area.

D Two plots of land with the same shape, the same perimeter and the same area.

Below are three solids of the same height: a regular square-based prism, a regular square-based pyramid and a right rectangular-based prism.

Solid A

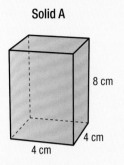

8 cm

4 cm
4 cm

Solid B

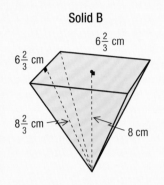

$6\frac{2}{3}$ cm

$6\frac{2}{3}$ cm

$8\frac{2}{3}$ cm

8 cm

Solid C

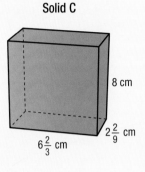

8 cm

$2\frac{2}{9}$ cm

$6\frac{2}{3}$ cm

a. Compare the surface area of Solid **A** to that of Solid **B**. What do you notice?

b. Solid **A** is completely filled with water. The water is then poured into to Solid **B**. Of the following choices, which best describes this situation?

❶ There is not enough water to completely fill Solid **B**.

❷ Solid **B** contains exactly as much water as Solid **A**.

❸ Water overflows out of Solid **B**.

c. Do two solids with the same surface area necessarily have the same volume? Explain your answer.

d. Compare the volume of Solid **B** to that of Solid **C**. What do you notice?

e. Solid **B** is covered with paper. The same amount of paper is then used to cover Solid **C**. Of the following choices, which best describes the situation?

❶ There is not enough paper to completely cover Solid **C**.

❷ Solid **C** requires exactly as much paper as Solid **B**.

❸ There is more paper than necessary to cover Solid **C**.

f. Do two solids with the same volume necessarily have the same surface area? Explain your answer.

Right prisms are found in the architecture, both ancient and modern, of downtown Montréal.

Techno math

Three-dimensional (3-D) dynamic geometry software allows you to determine the area of a plane figure and the volume of a solid. By using the tools TRIANGLE, CIRCLE, REGULAR PENTAGON, REGULAR OCTOGON, CUBE, PRISM, CYLINDER, AREA and VOLUME, you can display the area and volume of various figures.

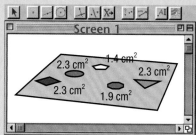

Using the plane figures on Screen **1** as a basis, it is possible to construct the solids found in Screen **2**.

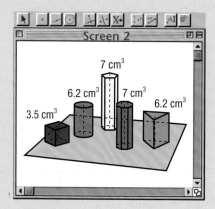

a. On Screen **1**:
   1) what is the circumference of the circle?
   2) what is the perimeter of the square?
   3) which plane figures have the same area?

b. On Screen **2**:
   1) what is the surface area of the cube?
   2) which solids have the same volume?
   3) which solids have the same volume and bases that have the same area?

c. Using 3-D dynamic geometry software, do the following:
   1) Draw a circle and two other plane figures, display their areas, and modify their dimensions until they all have the same area.
   2) Draw a sphere and two other solids, display their volumes, and modify their dimensions until they all have the same volume.

EQUIVALENT LINES

Two lines are equivalent if they are of the same length, regardless of their shape.

E.g. Since they are the same length, this segment and this arc of a circle are equivalent lines.

18 cm

18 cm

EQUIVALENT PLANE FIGURES

Two figures are equivalent if they have the same area, regardless of their shape.

E.g. Since they have the same area, this rectangle and this triangle are equivalent plane figures.

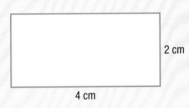

2 cm

4 cm

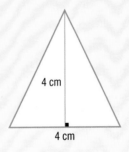

4 cm

4 cm

$$A_{\text{rectangle}} = 4 \times 2$$
$$A_{\text{rectangle}} = 8 \text{ cm}^2$$

$$A_{\text{triangle}} = \frac{4 \times 4}{2}$$
$$A_{\text{triangle}} = 8 \text{ cm}^2$$

EQUIVALENT SOLIDS

Two solids are equivalent if they have the same volume, regardless of their shape.

E.g. Since they have the same volume, this cube and this regular pyramid are equivalent solids.

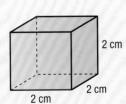

2 cm

2 cm

2 cm

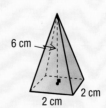

6 cm

2 cm

2 cm

$$V_{\text{cube}} = 2 \times 2 \times 2$$
$$V_{\text{cube}} = 8 \text{ cm}^3$$

$$V_{\text{pyramid}} = \frac{2 \times 2 \times 6}{3}$$
$$V_{\text{pyramid}} = 8 \text{ cm}^3$$

1 Match the pairs of equivalent figures.

A Rectangle

16 cm
10.89 cm

B Right triangle

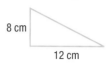
8 cm
12 cm

C Regular pentagon

10 m
6.88 m

D Equilateral triangle

3.46 cm

E Circle

16 cm

F Rectangle

20 cm
8.6 cm

G Parallelogram

12 cm
4 cm

H Isosceles triangle

3.46 cm
3.46 cm
30°

I Equilateral triangle

6 cm

J Square

13.2 m

2 Determine the perimeter that each of the following regular polygons must have to be considered equivalent to:

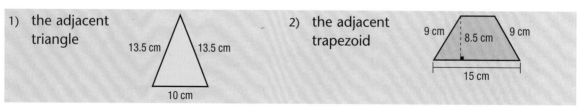

1) the adjacent triangle
13.5 cm   13.5 cm
10 cm

2) the adjacent trapezoid
9 cm   8.5 cm   9 cm
15 cm

a) equilateral triangle

b) square

c) regular pentagon

d) regular hexagon

e) regular heptagon

f) regular octagon

3   Identify the pairs of equivalent solids.

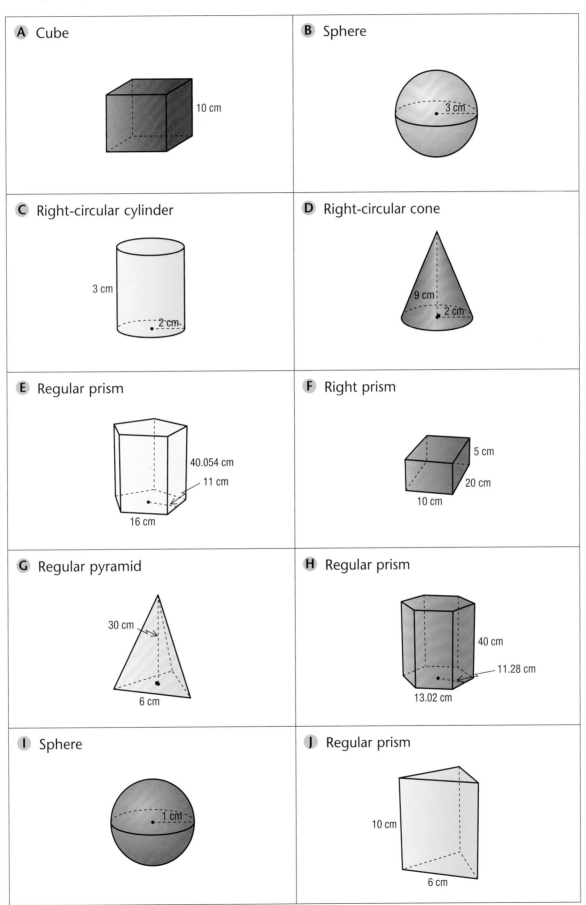

A   Cube

10 cm

B   Sphere

3 cm

C   Right-circular cylinder

3 cm

2 cm

D   Right-circular cone

9 cm

2 cm

E   Regular prism

40.054 cm

11 cm

16 cm

F   Right prism

5 cm

20 cm

10 cm

G   Regular pyramid

30 cm

6 cm

H   Regular prism

40 cm

11.28 cm

13.02 cm

I   Sphere

1 cm

J   Regular prism

10 cm

6 cm

4 A square and a circle are equivalent. If the square is made up of sides that measure 5 dm each, what is the circumference of the circle?

5 Below are the plans for two plots of land valued at $65/m².

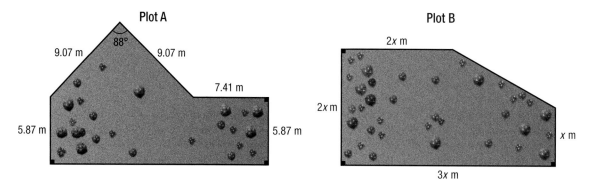

Plot A

88°
9.07 m   9.07 m
7.41 m
5.87 m   5.87 m

Plot B

2x m
2x m
x m
3x m

a) What is the area of Plot **A**?

b) What is the value of Plot **A**?

c) What is the length of each of Plot **B**'s sides if it is valued the same as that of Plot **A**?

6 A gardener uses two planks that are 2 m long and two planks that are 75 cm long to build a produce garden in the shape of a quadrilateral.

a) Explain why, in the space available for planting seedlings, he should create a garden that is in the shape of a quadrilateral that has right angles.

The table below displays the minimum space required for each type of plant.

Eggplant: 45 cm	Broccoli: 75 cm
Celery: 40 cm	Cabbage: 60 cm
Pumpkin: 90 cm	Romaine lettuce: 30 cm
Cantaloupe: 40 cm	Watermelon: 40 cm
Sweet potato: 45 cm	Red pepper: 30 cm
Tomato: 60 cm	Jerusalem artichoke: 60 cm

The sweet potato is not related to the potato! It is believed that this root vegetable originated in South America. It is a good source of vitamins A and D and is eaten cooked.

The Jerusalem artichoke is a resilient plant that is cultivated like a vegetable for its tubers. This kind, originating from North America, is popular in Europe. Its taste is similar to that of the heart of an artichoke.

b) For each produce plant listed above, determine the maximum number of plants that can be cultivated in a rectangular garden measuring 2 m by 75 cm.

7 There are plans to install one of the three following structures in a grass-covered yard.

Ⓐ A tool shed with a rectangular floor measuring 4 m by 3 m.

Ⓑ A play module with a rectangular base measuring 5 m by 2.5 m.

Ⓒ A tool shed with a floor in the shape of a regular octagon with sides measuring 1.5 m.

Which of the three structures should be installed so that the least amount of grass remains to be cut?

8 A company is specialized in tinting car windows. The rates vary based on the area of the window to be tinted.

Identify the pairs of windows that would cost the same amount to have tinted.

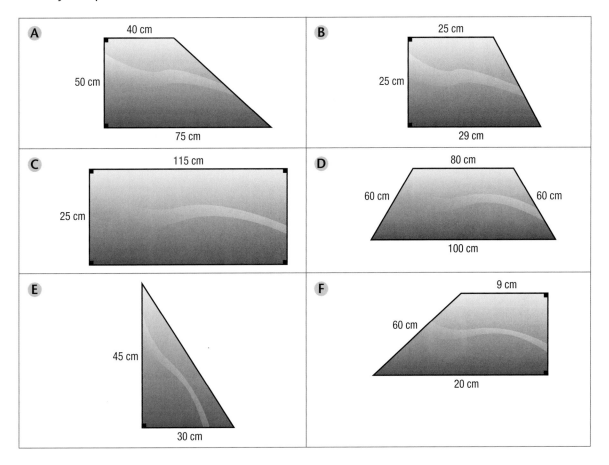

A
40 cm
50 cm
75 cm

B
25 cm
25 cm
29 cm

C
115 cm
25 cm

D
80 cm
60 cm   60 cm
100 cm

E
45 cm
30 cm

F
9 cm
60 cm
20 cm

The automobile industry has developed films that can be applied to windows in order to reduce overheating caused by solar radiation in summer and heat loss in winter.

9 In a fruit juice processing plant, a vat shaped as shown in the adjacent illustration is filled to the top with orange juice. After that, a certain amount of water is extracted to create a concentrate that will then be put in small containers. The following is some information about the transformation process:

- 1 dm³ is equivalent to 1 L.
- 1 cm³ is equivalent to 1 mL.
- The volume occupied by the concentrate is equivalent to 37.5% of the volume occupied by the juice.

a) How many litres of juice does the vat contain?

b) How many litres of concentrate will be put into containers?

c) The concentrate is packaged in 10 000 small containers in the shape of right circular cylinders with a height that is double the diameter of the base. What are the dimensions of one small container?

10 The two figures illustrated below are not equivalent.

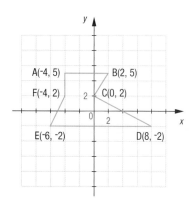 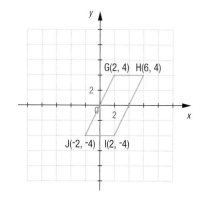

a) A dilatation centred at the origin is applied to:

1) figure ABCDEF. What is the scale factor if the figures A'B'C'D'E'F' and GHIJ are equivalent?

2) figure GHIJ. What is the scale factor if the figures G'H'I'J' and ABCDEF are equivalent?

b) A horizontal scale change is applied to:

1) figure ABCDEF. What is the transformation rule if the figures A'B'C'D'E'F' and GHIJ are equivalent?

2) figure GHIJ. What is the transformation rule if the figures G'H'I'J' and ABCDEF are equivalent?

c) A vertical scale change is applied to:

1) figure ABCDEF. What is the transformation rule if the figures A'B'C'D'E'F' and GHIJ are equivalent?

2) figure GHIJ. What is the transformation rule if the figures G'H'I'J' and ABCDEF are equivalent?

11 For each case, determine the perimeter of the polygon considering that it is equivalent to the adjacent circle.

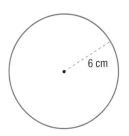

6 cm

a) Equilateral triangle

b) Square

c) Regular hexagon

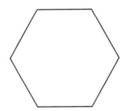

d) Regular octagon

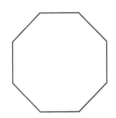

12 For each case, determine the missing length, considering that the solid is equivalent to the adjacent right-circular cone.

7.6 cm

2.9 cm

a) Right-circular cylinder

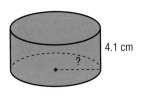

4.1 cm

?

b) Sphere

?

c) Right prism

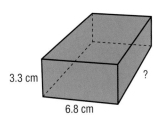

3.3 cm

?

6.8 cm

d) Regular pyramid

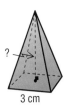

?

3 cm

This section is related to LES 5 and 6.

PROBLEM In top shape!

In a factory specializing in making food containers, a foreman meets with the design team. Taking various criteria into account, this team determines, among other things, the shape of the container and the materials that are used to make it.

WE HAVE TO THINK OF THE BEST SHAPE A ONE LITRE MILK CONTAINER, TO MINIMIZE PRODUCTION COSTS, WE HAVE TO USE THE LEAST AMOUNT OF MATERIAL POSSIBLE

IN THAT CASE, WE SHOULD JUST PICK THE NICEST SHAPE FOR A CONTAINER!

WHY ALL THE DRAMA? NO MATTER WHAT THE SHAPE OF THE CONTAINER, THE AMOUNT OF MATERIAL NEEDED TO MAKE IT WILL ALWAYS BE THE SAME.

THE CONTAINER SHOULD BE IN THE SHAPE OF A CUBE. IT IS THE SHAPE THAT WOULD REQUIRE THE LEAST AMOUNT OF MATERIALS TO PRODUCE.

I WONDER IF A SPHERE WOULD BE THE MOST EFFICIENT SHAPE.

A SPHERE REALLY ISN'T A SUITABLE SHAPE FOR TRANSPORTING HUNDREDS OF CONTAINERS.

A PYRAMID OR A CYLINDER WOULD BE ORIGINAL!

IT HAS TO BE EASY TO HOLD WHEN YOU POUR FROM IT AND IT HAS TO FIT NICELY IN A REFRIGERATOR.

Which shape of container would you choose?

Below are a few non-congruent triangles.

Triangle Ⓐ

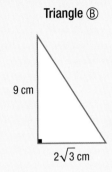

Triangle Ⓑ

9 cm

2√3 cm

Triangle Ⓒ

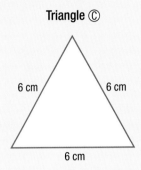

a. Verify that these triangles are equivalent.

b. Calculate the perimeter of each of the triangles.

Below are a few non-congruent rectangles.

Rectangle Ⓐ

36 cm

1 cm

Rectangle Ⓑ

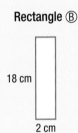

18 cm

2 cm

Rectangle Ⓒ

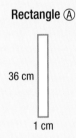

12 cm

3 cm

Rectangle Ⓓ

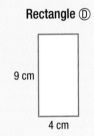

9 cm

4 cm

Rectangle Ⓔ

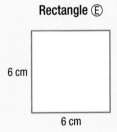

6 cm

6 cm

c. Verify that these rectangles are equivalent.

d. Calculate the perimeter of each of the rectangles.

e. What conjecture can you formulate regarding the perimeter of all equivalent polygons with the same number of sides?

Below is a series of equivalent polygons.

Number of sides	3	4	8	12
Polygon	Equilateral triangle ≈ 6.8 cm	Rectangle 5 cm, 4 cm	Regular octagon ≈ 2.04 cm	Regular dodecagon ≈ 1.34 cm
Perimeter (cm)	≈ 20.4	18	≈ 16.32	≈ 16.08

f. What is the area of each of these equivalent polygons?

g. As the number of sides increases:
1) what can you say about the perimeter?
2) what figure does this series of polygons begin to resemble?

h. What is the perimeter of the figure that this series of polygons resembles?

i. What conjecture can you formulate regarding the perimeter of two equivalent polygons with different numbers of sides?

Below are a few non-congruent right rectangular-based prisms.

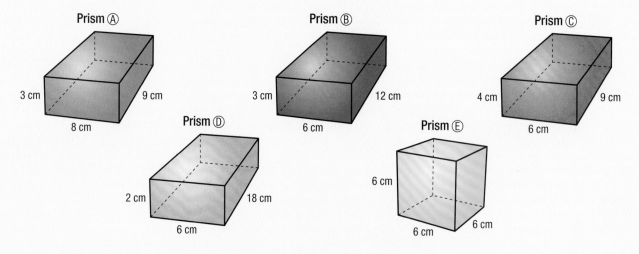

Prism Ⓐ — 3 cm, 9 cm, 8 cm

Prism Ⓑ — 3 cm, 12 cm, 6 cm

Prism Ⓒ — 4 cm, 9 cm, 6 cm

Prism Ⓓ — 2 cm, 18 cm, 6 cm

Prism Ⓔ — 6 cm, 6 cm, 6 cm

j. Verify that the prisms are equivalent.

k. Calculate the surface area of each of these prisms.

l. What conjecture can you formulate regarding the surface area of all equivalent right rectangular-based prisms?

Below is a series of equivalent polyhedrons:

Number of faces	6	8	12	20
Polyhedron	Cube	Regular octahedron	Regular dodecahedron	Regular icosahedron
	6 cm			
Surface area (cm²)	216	≈ 205.89	≈ 191.22	≈ 185.34

m. What is the volume of each of the equivalent polyhedrons?

n. As the number of faces increases:
1) what can you say about the surface area?
2) what solid does this series of polyhedrons begin to resemble?

o. What is the surface area of the equivalent solid that this series of polyhedrons resembles?

Below is a series of polyhedrons with equal surface area.

Number of faces	6	8	12	20
Solid	Cube	Regular octahedron	Regular dodecahedron	Regular icosahedron
	6 cm			
Volume (cm³)	216	≈ 232.11	≈ 259.32	≈ 271.76

p. What is the surface area of each of the polyhedrons?

q. As the number of faces increases:
1) what can you say about the volume?
2) what solid does this series of polyhedrons begin to resemble?

r. What is the volume of the solid that this series of polyhedrons resembles?

COMPARING EQUIVALENT PLANE FIGURES

- Of all equivalent polygons with *n* sides, the regular polygon has the smallest perimeter.

E.g. Comparing the perimeters *P* and the areas *A* of two quadrilaterals

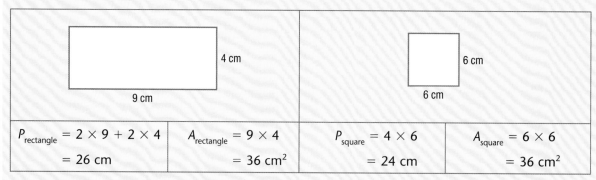

$P_{rectangle}$ = 2 × 9 + 2 × 4	$A_{rectangle}$ = 9 × 4	P_{square} = 4 × 6	A_{square} = 6 × 6
= 26 cm	= 36 cm²	= 24 cm	= 36 cm²

Since they have the same area, these two quadrilaterals are equivalent. However, the perimeter of a regular quadrilateral, the square, is smaller than that of an irregular quadrilateral, the rectangle.

- Between two equivalent convex polygons, the polygon with the greatest number of sides has the smallest perimeter.

E.g. Comparing the perimeters *P* and areas *A* of two polygons

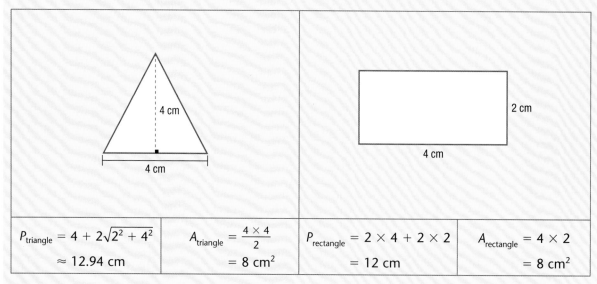

$P_{triangle}$ = 4 + 2$\sqrt{2^2 + 4^2}$	$A_{triangle}$ = $\dfrac{4 \times 4}{2}$	$P_{rectangle}$ = 2 × 4 + 2 × 2	$A_{rectangle}$ = 4 × 2
≈ 12.94 cm	= 8 cm²	= 12 cm	= 8 cm²

Since they have the same area, these two polygons are equivalent. However, the perimeter of the polygon with the most sides, the rectangle, is smaller than that of the polygon with fewer sides, the triangle.

It should be noted that of all the equivalent plane figures, the circle has the smallest perimeter.

COMPARING SOLIDS WITH THE SAME SURFACE AREA

- Of all rectangular prisms with the same surface area, the cube has the greatest volume.

E.g. Comparing the surface areas A and volumes V of two rectangular prisms

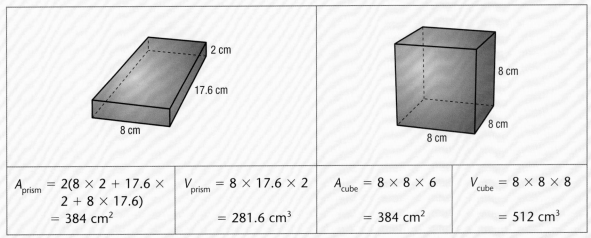

| $A_{prism} = 2(8 \times 2 + 17.6 \times 2 + 8 \times 17.6)$ $= 384 \text{ cm}^2$ | $V_{prism} = 8 \times 17.6 \times 2$ $= 281.6 \text{ cm}^3$ | $A_{cube} = 8 \times 8 \times 6$ $= 384 \text{ cm}^2$ | $V_{cube} = 8 \times 8 \times 8$ $= 512 \text{ cm}^3$ |

Even though these two rectangular prisms have the same surface area, the cube has the greater volume.

- Of all solids with the same surface area, the sphere has the greatest volume.

E.g. Comparing the surface areas A and volumes V of two solids

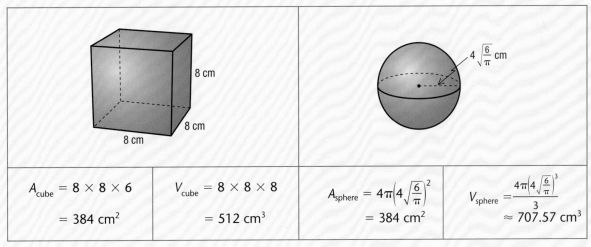

| $A_{cube} = 8 \times 8 \times 6$ $= 384 \text{ cm}^2$ | $V_{cube} = 8 \times 8 \times 8$ $= 512 \text{ cm}^3$ | $A_{sphere} = 4\pi\left(4\sqrt{\dfrac{6}{\pi}}\right)^2$ $= 384 \text{ cm}^2$ | $V_{sphere} = \dfrac{4\pi\left(4\sqrt{\dfrac{6}{\pi}}\right)^3}{3}$ $\approx 707.57 \text{ cm}^3$ |

Even though these two solids have the same surface area, the sphere has the greater volume.

COMPARING EQUIVALENT SOLIDS

- Of all equivalent rectangular prisms, the cube has the smallest surface area.

E.g. Comparing the surface areas A and volumes V of two rectangular prisms

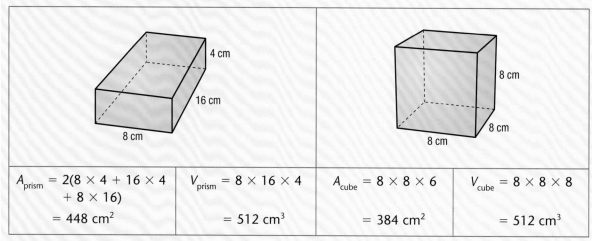

$A_{prism} = 2(8 \times 4 + 16 \times 4 + 8 \times 16)$ $= 448 \text{ cm}^2$	$V_{prism} = 8 \times 16 \times 4$ $= 512 \text{ cm}^3$	$A_{cube} = 8 \times 8 \times 6$ $= 384 \text{ cm}^2$	$V_{cube} = 8 \times 8 \times 8$ $= 512 \text{ cm}^3$

Since they have the same volume, these two rectangular prisms are equivalent. However, the cube has the smaller surface area.

- Of all equivalent solids, the sphere has the smallest surface area.

E.g. Comparing the surface areas A and volumes V of two solids

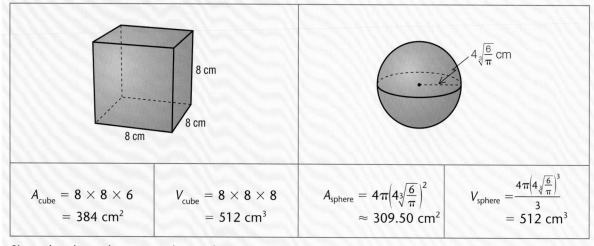

$A_{cube} = 8 \times 8 \times 6$ $= 384 \text{ cm}^2$	$V_{cube} = 8 \times 8 \times 8$ $= 512 \text{ cm}^3$	$A_{sphere} = 4\pi\left(4\sqrt[3]{\dfrac{6}{\pi}}\right)^2$ $\approx 309.50 \text{ cm}^2$	$V_{sphere} = \dfrac{4\pi\left(4\sqrt[3]{\dfrac{6}{\pi}}\right)^3}{3}$ $= 512 \text{ cm}^3$

Since they have the same volume, these two solids are equivalent. However, the sphere has the smaller surface area.

1 Place these nine equivalent regular polygons in increasing order based on their perimeter.

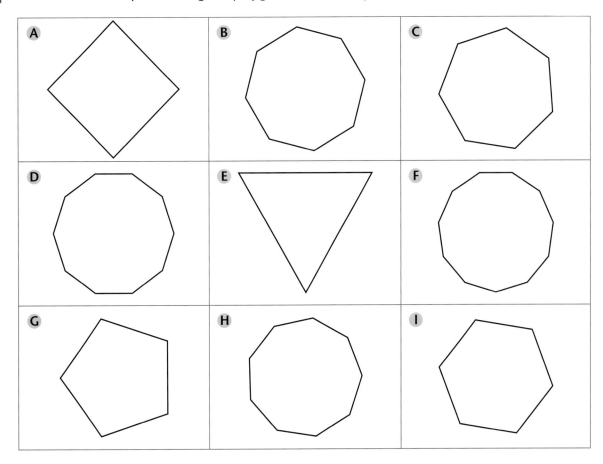

2 Place these six equivalent solids in decreasing order based on their surface area.

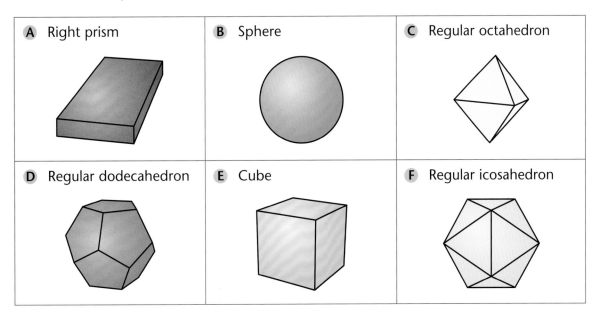

3 A manufacturer of a new board game must wrap four dice together in plastic wrap. The manufacturer can wrap the dice in one of the two following configurations.

Wrapper A

Wrapper B

Which of the two wrappers requires less plastic?

4 A polyethylene sheet is used to wrap a package of 8 pieces of fibreglass insulation. Considering that fibreglass insulation can lose up to 40% of its volume when it is compressed and wrapped, what is the area of the smallest polyethylene sheet capable of wrapping a package of 8 pieces of fibreglass insulation based on the dimensions provided below?

Dimensions of an unwrapped piece of fibreglass insulation

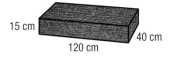

15 cm
40 cm
120 cm

Fibreglass insulation is used in the building industry for thermal insulation.

5 A printing plant wraps books in packages of 12 using plastic before distributing them to bookstores. What is the minimum area of plastic film that could be used to wrap 12 books that are 18.5 cm wide, 23 cm long and 3.5 cm thick?

In the West, Gutenberg is known for developing modern typography and introducing the printing press (1440). Each line of text had to be composed manually using mobile letters made out of lead.

The use of new reproduction techniques has evolved over the centuries. Towards 1880, the printer was re-invented with the invention of linotype, where each line of text could be entered with a keyboard. Today, it is the offset press that produces the greatest volume of printing.

6 A confectioner makes little chocolates coated in a candy shell 1 mm thick. Each little chocolate is prepared with 2.5 g of chocolate and is shaped into one of the solids shown below.

Right circular cylinder with a diameter of 1 cm

Cube

Sphere

The country that consumes the most chocolate annually is Switzerland, at 10.74 kg for each inhabitant. Canadians annually consume 3.9 kg of chocolate for each inhabitant.

Below is some information about the chocolate and the candy coating:

- 1 mL of chocolate has a mass of 0.8 g and a volume of 1 cm³.
- The confectioner has 1000 kg of chocolate.
- The confectioner spends $2.50 to buy 1 L of candy coating.

a) How many little chocolates can the confectioner make?

b) How much candy coating is used to cover a little chocolate that is in the shape of a:
   1) cylinder?   2) cube?   3) sphere?

c) How much does the confectioner save by making little chocolates in the shape of a sphere rather than in the shape of a:
   1) cylinder?   2) cube?

7 Twenty-four cylindrical cans with a diameter of 8 cm and a height of 11 cm are to be put in a box.

a) In ascending order, rank the four possible configurations shown according to:
   1) the area of cardboard needed to make each of the boxes
   2) the unoccupied volume in each of the boxes

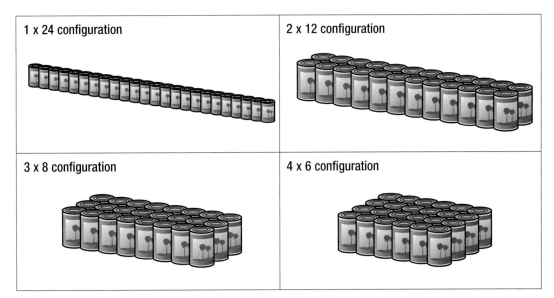

1 x 24 configuration

2 x 12 configuration

3 x 8 configuration

4 x 6 configuration

b) Considering that each of the cans has a mass of 750 g and that 1 cm² of cardboard has a mass of 1 g, rank, in ascending order, the four possible configurations shown according to the total mass of each of the boxes.

8 The adjacent diagram illustrates a plot of land on which several greenhouses, each covering a surface of 11 m², are to be built. What is the maximum number of identically shaped greenhouses that can be built on this land?

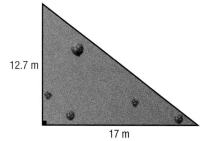

Opened in 1958, Montréal's Botanical Garden's greenhouses cover a surface of 4000 m². Each of the 10 greenhouses has a particular theme: ferns, arid regions, bonsais, humid tropical regions, etc. All together, there are approximately 36 000 plants.

9 A person makes cushions. What is the volume of the largest cushion the person can make using 2.25 m² of fabric?

10 An uninflated balloon is placed in a cubic box with 18-cm edges. The balloon is then inflated until it takes on the shape of the box.

a) At that moment:

   1) how much air (in mL) is in the balloon?

   2) what is the surface area of the balloon?

The box is taken apart to free the balloon. The balloon then takes on a spherical shape.

b) At that moment:

   1) how much air (in mL) is in the balloon?

   2) what is the area of the balloon?

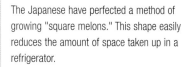

The Japanese have perfected a method of growing "square melons." This shape easily reduces the amount of space taken up in a refrigerator.

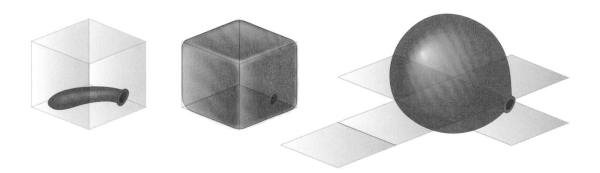

11 A plastic moulding company makes compost bins. What is the maximum number of 35-L bins that can be made from 1000 L of plastic, if the sides of the bins are 5 mm thick?

12 A person must choose among the three following tiling patterns to cover a 1.5-m by 3-m rectangular section of bathroom floor.

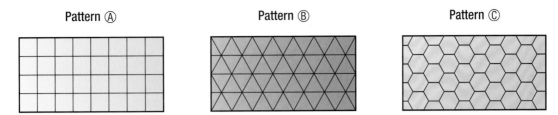

Pattern Ⓐ   Pattern Ⓑ   Pattern Ⓒ

The space between the tiles is filled with cement made for that purpose. Which of these patterns requires the least amount of cement? Justify your answer.

13 A temporary car shelter is installed over a 5-m by 12-m rectangular entrance. What is the smallest area of canvas required to cover the shelter if the tallest part of the shelter is 2.5 m above the ground?

14 Making a battery cell requires combining at least two chemical components in a metal casing whose lateral surfaces are covered with a label. The top and bottom faces of the casing are the battery's terminals. A battery-maker must decide among four different battery formats, all with the same volume.

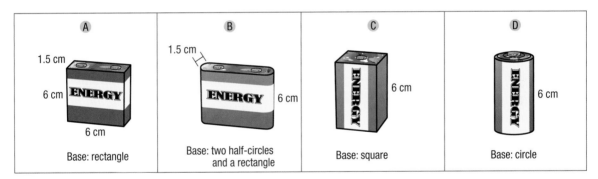

A
1.5 cm
6 cm ENERGY
6 cm
Base: rectangle

B
1.5 cm
ENERGY
6 cm
Base: two half-circles and a rectangle

C
6 cm
ENERGY
Base: square

D
6 cm
ENERGY
Base: circle

Of the four formats, which should the maker choose to ensure that labelling costs are at a minimum? Explain your answer.

A battery cell is a device that transforms the energy produced by a chemical reaction into electrical energy.

Michel Chasles
(1793-1880)

His life

Michel Chasles was a French mathematician born in Épernon. After excelling in high school, he entered Paris' École polytechnique in 1812 and went on to become a professor there in 1841. In 1846, the position of Chair of Higher Geometry was created for him at the Sorbonne, a renowned university.

His specialty

Michel Chasles worked in several areas of mathematics but particularly in projective geometry. This type of geometry deals with viewing objects from a point in space. Chasles invented the French term *homothétie*, which means *dilatation*, as well as the expression *similar figures*.

Projective geometry deals with dilatation.
Below are two examples of projections.

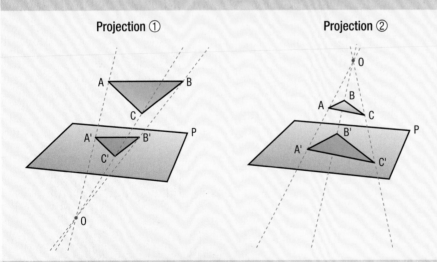

Each projection displays, on plane P, the result of triangle ABC seen from point O. In each case, the triangles ABC and A'B'C' are similar.

Michel Chasles' name is among the 72 names of reknowned people engraved on the four facades of the Eiffel Tower.

The Chasles relation

Chasles worked a great deal on the mathematical concept known as "vector." An important vector relation is the Chasles relation, which in a way, corresponds to a series of translations in a plane. Below are two examples:

Example ①

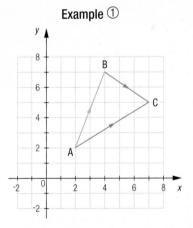

A translation that associates point A with point B, followed by a translation that associates point B with point C is equivalent to a single translation, meaning the one that associates point A with point C.

Example ②

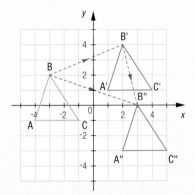

Translation $t_{(5, 2)}$ followed by translation $t_{(1, -4)}$ is equivalent to translation $t_{(6, -2)}$.

1. Consider points A(2,0), B(7, 13), C(4, -5) and D(3, 1). Find a single translation that is equivalent to the following:

a) a translation that associates point A with point B, followed by a translation that associates point B with point C

b) a translation that associates point A with point B, followed by a translation that associates point B with point C, followed by a translation that associates point C with point D

2. Find a single translation that is equivalent to:

a) translation $t_{(2, -6)}$ followed by translation $t_{(5, 1)}$

b) translation $t_{(4, 9)}$ followed by translation $t_{(3, -1)}$

c) translation $t_{(4, 5)}$ followed by translation $t_{(-2, 5)}$, followed by translation $t_{(-2, -10)}$

3. Complete the projection of triangle ABC onto plane P in relation to point O.

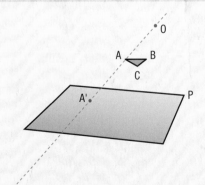

Different possibilities

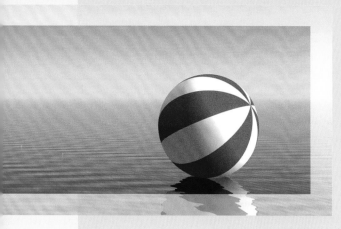

3-D animation and image synthesis technicians are creative individuals with an excellent artistic sense and an ability to translate an idea or a concept into a visual representation. They are called upon to work in various areas, including comic strip design, scriptwriting, character animation, special effects and three-dimensional (3-D) backgrounds. The multimedia, entertainment and advertising industries are increasingly hiring 3-D animation and image synthesis technicians.

3-D imagery and geometric transformations

Most 3-D animations start with two-dimensional (2-D) figures which, by means of projections involving translations, rotations and dilatations, become representations of polyhedrons.

Below is how a 3-D animation and image synthesis technician would go about producing a torus, commonly known as a "doughnut."

Transformations
▷ Translation
▷ +90° rotation
▷ -90° rotation
▷ 180° rotation
▷ Dilatation

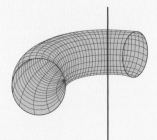

The initial figure is a circle.

The circle turns in space around an axis of rotation.

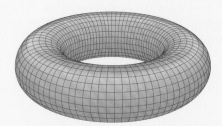

Once the rotation is complete, you obtain a torus.

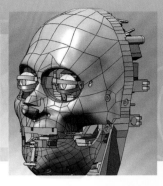

Motion capture

In order for the motion of synthetic images to look as natural as possible, 3-D animation and image synthesis technicians use motion capture, a technique wherein an actor moves around while wearing several sensors whose positions are recorded in three dimensions and processed by image creation software.

Montréal is a worldwide hub for the design and production of video games of various types.

1. Describe the geometric transformation a 3-D animation and image synthesis technician would have to use to generate each of the solids starting with the initial figure given.

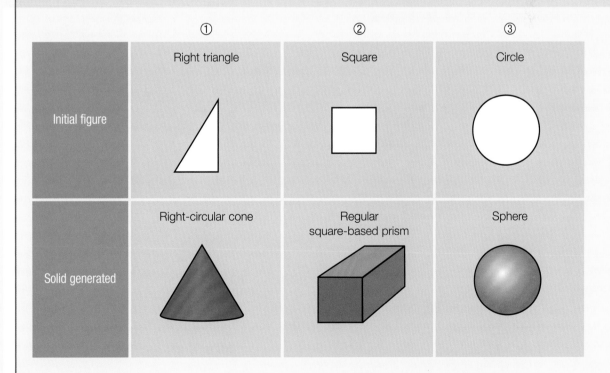

	①	②	③
	Right triangle	Square	Circle
Initial figure			
	Right-circular cone	Regular square-based prism	Sphere
Solid generated			

overview

1 For each case, determine the rule that associates the initial point with its image considering the geometric transformation indicated.

a) A(20, 16) and A'(-5, -4) by dilatation.

b) B(11, -18) and B'(11, -9) by reduction.

c) C(-15, 15) and C'(-15, -15) by reflection.

d) D(14, 1) and D'(-1, 14) by rotation.

e) E(-7, 17) and E'(7, 17) by reflection.

f) F(4, 17) and F'(16, 17) by horizontal stretch.

2 In the adjacent graph, which geometric transformation associates figures:

a) A and B?

b) A and C?

c) A and D?

d) B and D?

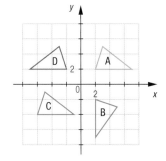

3 For each case, do the following:

> 1) Identify the transformation rule that associates the two polygons.
>
> 2) Determine the coordinates of the vertices B' and C'.

a)

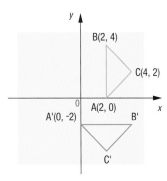

b)

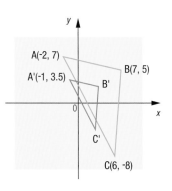

c)

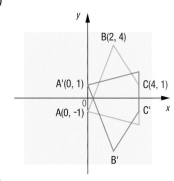

d)

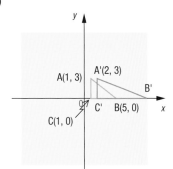

e)

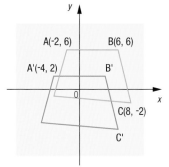

f)

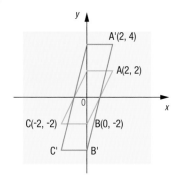

4 Each of the polyhedrons below has a volume of 18.5 cm³. Which has the smallest surface area? Explain your answer.

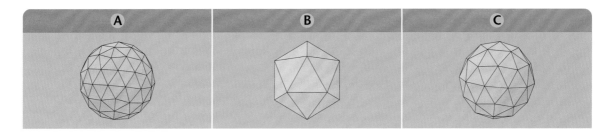

5 Determine the values of *a, b, c, d* and *e* if all the regular polygons below are equivalent.

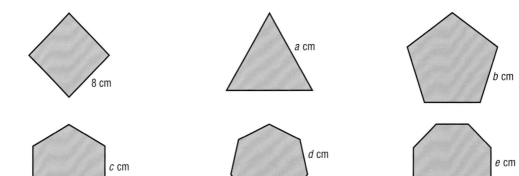

8 cm

a cm

b cm

c cm

d cm

e cm

6 For each case shown below, determine the transformation rule that associates the two curves.

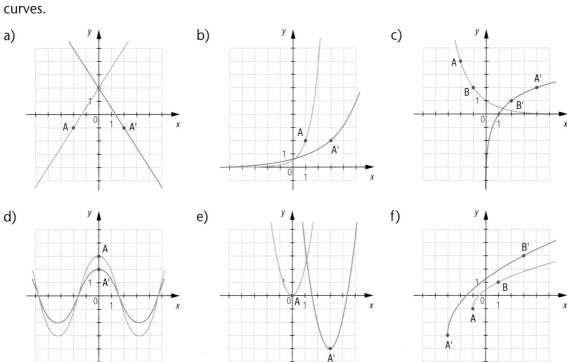

a)

b)

c)

d)

e)

f)

7 A box must be made to hold the vase shown below. Among the boxes suggested in the table, which would require the least amount of material to make? Explain your answer.

Box	Box characteristics
Ⓐ	Solid: right prism Height: 18 cm Base: rectangle with sides measuring 12 cm by 10.39 cm
Ⓑ	Solid: regular prism Height: 18 cm Base: square with sides measuring 12 cm
Ⓒ	Solid: regular prism Height: 18 cm Base: regular hexagon with sides measuring 6 cm
Ⓓ	Solid: right-circular cylinder Height: 18 cm Base: circle with radius measuring 6 cm
Ⓔ	Solid: right-circular cylinder Height: 18 cm Base: circle with radius measuring 5.2 cm

Regular prism with hexagonal base

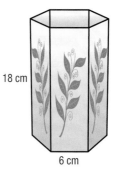

18 cm

6 cm

8 For each case, determine the unknown measurement that would result in equivalent solids.

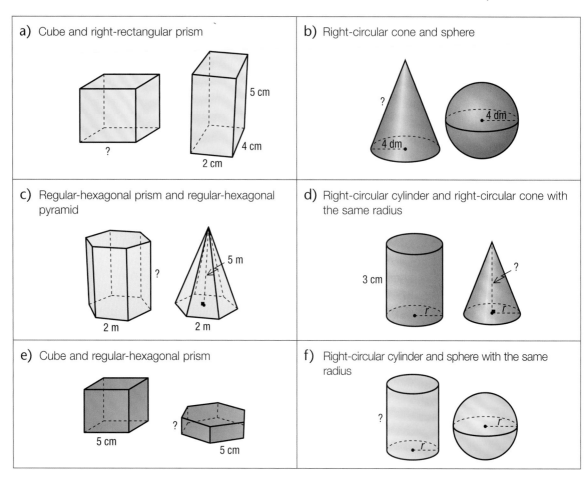

a) Cube and right-rectangular prism

5 cm
4 cm
2 cm
?

b) Right-circular cone and sphere

?
4 dm
4 dm

c) Regular-hexagonal prism and regular-hexagonal pyramid

?
5 m
2 m
2 m

d) Right-circular cylinder and right-circular cone with the same radius

3 cm
?
r
r

e) Cube and regular-hexagonal prism

5 cm
?
5 cm

f) Right-circular cylinder and sphere with the same radius

?
r
r

9 Complete the following tables.

a)

Initial point	Image under translation $t_{(7, -1)}$
A(7, -2)	A'(,)
B(0, 3)	B'(,)
C(1, 4)	C'(,)

b)

Initial point	Image under rotation $r_{(O, -90°)}$
D(3, -8)	D'(,)
E(10, 9)	E'(,)
F(5, 5)	F'(,)

c)

Initial point	Image under reflection s_y
G(3, -1)	G'(,)
H(5, -2)	H'(,)
I(2, 2)	I'(,)

d)

Initial point	Image under dilatation $h_{(O, 3)}$
J(0, 0)	J'(,)
K(2, 2)	K'(,)
L(4, -1)	L'(,)

e)

Initial point	Image under dilatation $h_{(O, -3.9)}$
M(3, 8)	M'(,)
N(0, 10)	N'(,)
O(9, -4)	O'(,)

f)

Initial point	Image under horizontal stretch $(x, y) \mapsto (2.3x, y)$
P(-3, 6)	P'(,)
Q(0, 4)	Q'(,)
R(4, -2)	R'(,)

10 The points A(-2, 1), B(3, 4) and C(4, -2) are the vertices of a triangle. The area of triangle ABC is 16.5 mm², and its perimeter is approximately 18.62 mm. For each of the transformations below, calculate:

1) the area of the image

2) the perimeter of the image

a) $t_{(-2, -1)}$

b) s_x

c) $r_{(O, -90°)}$

d) $h_{(O, 1.5)}$

e) $(x, y) \mapsto (x, 2y)$

f) $(x, y) \mapsto (2x, y)$

11 Complete the table below.

Geometric transformation	$\dfrac{\text{area of image}}{\text{area of initial figure}}$	Are the initial figure and its image equivalent: yes or no?
Translation		
Rotation		
Reflection		
$h_{(O, 2)}$		
$h_{(O, 0.5)}$		
$(x, y) \mapsto (x, 2y)$		
$(x, y) \mapsto (2x, y)$		
$(x, y) \mapsto (x, 0.5y)$		
$(x, y) \mapsto (0.5x, y)$		

12 For each of the geometric transformations below, complete the following table.

Transformation rule	Description	Initial figure and image
a)	Add 1 unit to the x-coordinates and a subtract of 5 units from the y-coordinates.	
b)		
c)	Multiply the x-coordinate by 3.	
d)		
e)		

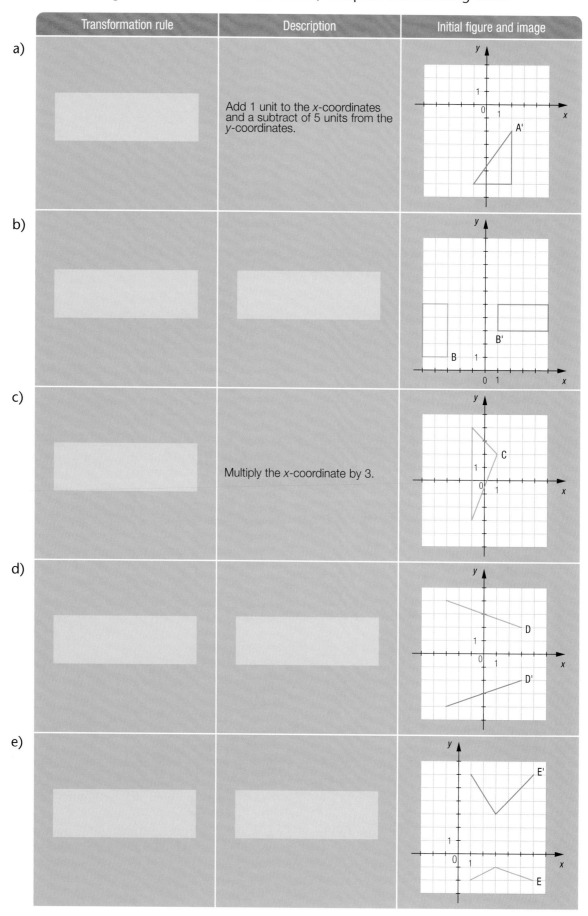

13 For each case, two successive geometric transformations, starting from the initial figure, were performed to obtain an image. For each graph, determine two rules for successive transformations that would associate the two figures.

a)

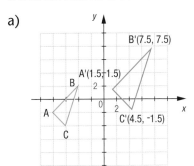

b)

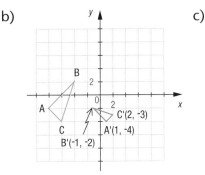

c)

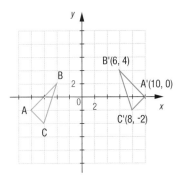

d)

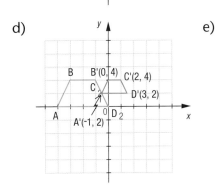

e)

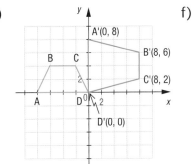

f)

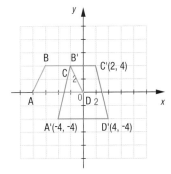

14 A children's toy manufacurer wants to wrap packages of 24 pieces of wood, as shown in the adjacent illustration, using plastic film. What is the area of the smallest wrapper that would suffice?

Right prism with bases that are isosceles trapezoids

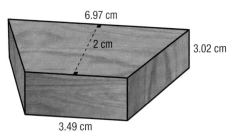

6.97 cm

2 cm

3.02 cm

3.49 cm

15 The following is a table of values for function f where $f(x) = 2x^2$.

Function f

x	-3	-2	-1	0	1	2	3
f(x)	18	8	2	0	2	8	18

a) The rule of function g is $g(x) = -2x^2$. Complete the table of values below.

Function g

x	-3	-2	-1	0	1	2	3
g(x)	■	■	■	■	■	■	■

b) In comparing the ordered pairs in the tables of values for functions f and g, what do you notice?

c) Draw the curves associated with functions f and g in the same Cartesian plane.

d) Which geometric transformation would associate the curves of these two functions?

16 Draw the figure associated with the triangle below resulting from a reflection about:

a) the line with equation $y = x$

b) the line with equation $y = -x$

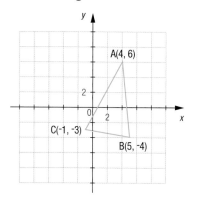

17 a) For each pair of points, determine two rules that would map the initial point onto the image.

1) A(7, -5) and A'(-5, -7)
2) B(-2, 5) and B'(-8, 20)
3) C(5, 5) and C'(5, 1)
4) D(4, 14) and D'(-12, 14)
5) E(13, 19) and E'(-13, -19)
6) F(-1, 3) and F'(1, 3)

b) What conjecture can you formulate based on the answers obtained in **a)**?

18 A plastic moulding factory has four compost bin models that have airholes distributed over their surface.

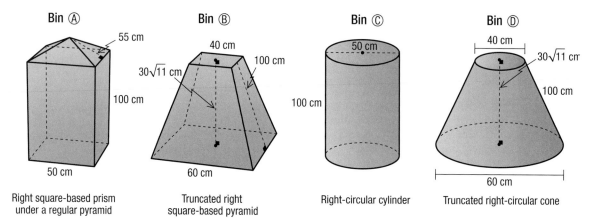

Bin Ⓐ
Right square-based prism under a regular pyramid

Bin Ⓑ
Truncated right square-based pyramid

Bin Ⓒ
Right-circular cylinder

Bin Ⓓ
Truncated right-circular cone

These models of compost bins do not have a bottom. The compost sits directly on the ground.

The bins that have the largest surface exposed to air allow for better ventilation of the compost and a more favourable exposure to the sun, which accelerates the composting process.

From the model bins shown above, which:

a) has the most favourable ventilation airway for the compost?

b) requires the least amount of plastic to create?

c) can contain the largest amount of compost?

19 The adjacent illustration shows the pattern of a soccer ball created using congruent regular hexagons and congruent regular pentagons. The area of the pattern is 1560 cm². Once assembled and before inflated, the ball is in the form of a polyhedron.

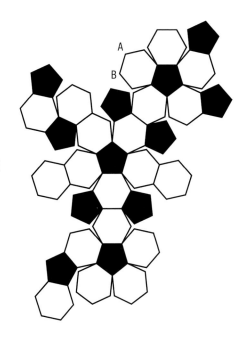

a) What is the length of segment AB, considering that the apothem of the hexagon is 4.01 cm and that of the pentagon is 3.19 cm?

b) Once inflated, the ball is in the form of a sphere. Calculate the volume of air that is contained in the ball.

c) Based on FIFA requirements, a soccer ball has to have a circumference between 68 cm and 70 cm. Does this soccer ball meet the requirements? Explain your answer.

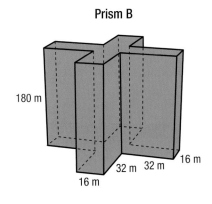

The architectural design of the dome at the Biosphere on Île Sainte-Helene in Montréal is based on triangles.

Since 1996, only soccer balls that pass the requirements set by the *Fédération Internationale de Football Association* (FIFA) are usable in international competitions organized by FIFA.

20 Below are two right prisms:

Prism A

Prism B

180 m

180 m

48 m

48 m

180 m

32 m 32 m 16 m

16 m

Place Ville-Marie in Montréal is a cross-shaped building: the aerial view is in the shape of a cross. This configuration is advantageous because it offers more natural light for the same amount of floor space than a square building.

a) Are these prisms equivalent?

b) Are the bases of these prisms equivalent?

c) How many times bigger is the lateral area of Prism **B** than the lateral area of Prism **A**?

bank of problems

 1 As shown in the illustration below, a company makes cookies in the form of octagonal-based regular prisms. Each side of the base of this cookie measures 2.5 cm, and the cookie is 4 mm thick. The company makes packages of 20 cookies. How should these cookies be placed so that the least amount of packaging is used?

Gingerbread is a molasses cake flavored with various spices. In countries where Christmas is celebrated, it is considered to be a festive cake and is found in various forms. The best known form is that of a "gingerbread man."

 2 Using a Cartesian plane, Gina applies rotation $r_{(O, 90°)}$ followed by translation $t_{(8, 4)}$. Frank claims that the same outcome would result by applying translation $t_{(4, -8)}$ followed by rotation $r_{(O, 90°)}$. Algebraically, confirm or refute Frank's claim.

 3 **PROJECTING IMAGES** Images of various formats can be projected onto a screen. The ratio $\frac{\text{horizontal dimension}}{\text{vertical dimension}}$ of an image or screen is used to define their format.

Traditionally, films were captured in a 4:3 format. To project this type of film onto a screen with a 16:9 format, an image converter is used. Explain to an image technician how to convert the horizontal dimensions of a 4:3 format to fill a screen with a 16:9 format.

 4 Transformation geometry is applied to a Cartesian plane that contains convex quadrilateral ABCD. Below is some information about this:

• The coordinates of the vertices of the initial figure are (12, 4), (-1, -6), (8, -2) and (9, 6) respectively.

• The coordinates of the vertices of the image are (-27, 12), (-36, 8), (3, -12) and (-24, -4) respectively.

What geometric transformation was applied to this Cartesian plane?

5 The adjacent illustration shows a plastic storage box in the form of a rectangular-based prism. What would be the dimensions of a box that has the same volume as this box but whose view from above would correspond to the illustration below?

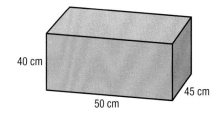

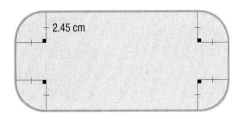

6 Cartoon animation often requires geometric transformations. To create the illusion of movement, a cartoonist uses Figure ① shown below and applies numerous geometric transformations.

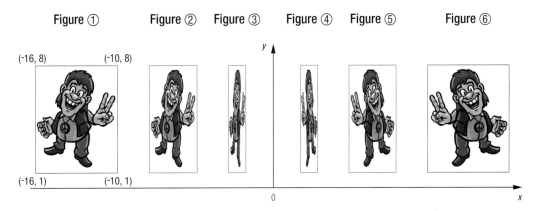

In this Cartesian plane, the following can be noted:

- The ratio of the areas of Figure ① to Figure ② is 2, and the ratio of the areas of Figure ① to Figure ③ is 6.

- The initial figure and all of image figures are the same height.

- Figures ① and ⑥ are congruent, Figures ② and ⑤ are congruent, and Figures ③ and ④ are congruent.

Determine five rules that associate Figures ②, ③, ④, ⑤ and ⑥ with Figure ①.

Shrek, an American movie filmed using synthesis imaging, is an adaptation of a classic fairy tale. It won the 2001 Academy Award for Best Animated Feature.

7 The illustration below shows the interior of a coffee maker that is in the shape of a truncated-regular pyramid.

What are the dimensions of a truncated-circular cone that is equivalent to the solid illustrated below and is also the same height?

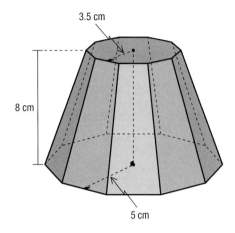

3.5 cm

8 cm

5 cm

In its classic form, the coffee maker, or *cafetiera*, is made up of two truncated-regular pyramids joined together by a cylindrical part.

8 Design software is becoming more popular in creating artistic work. The drawing below was created by applying successive geometric transformations on an initial figure. Determine the rule that associates these two figures.

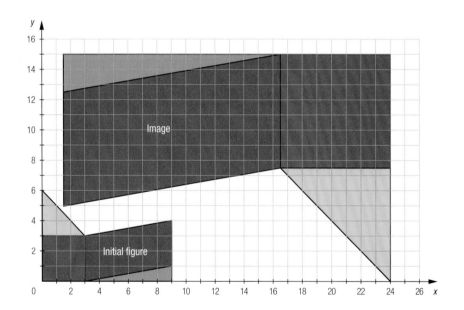

9 In a Cartesian plane, two sides of a parallelogram ABCD are parallel to the *x*-axis. A geometric transformation is applied whose rule is $(x, y) \mapsto \left(kx, \dfrac{y}{k}\right)$ where k is a non-zero number. Algebraically, show that figure ABCD and A'B'C'D' are equivalent figures.

10 Describe the succession of geometric transformations that associate the two figures shown below.

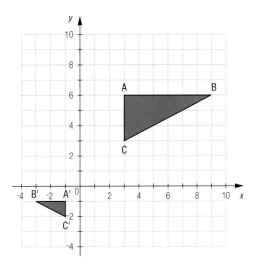

11 Formulate and validate a conjecture for the person who is correct.

I PILE MY CLOTHES BEFORE PUTTING THEM INTO MY SUITCASE. THEY TAKE UP LESS SPACE WHEN I DO IT THIS WAY.

I ROLL MY CLOTHES BEFORE PUTTING THEM INTO MY SUITCASE. THEY TAKE UP LESS SPACE WHEN I DO IT THIS WAY.

LEARNING AND EVALUATION SITUATIONS

TABLE OF CONTENTS

✱ Electronic media

○ Learning context

Since the advent of the Internet, the world of media has undergone enormous changes. Paper media have given way to electronic media. For example, researchers do their research on the Internet rather than in the paper versions of magazines, dictionaries or encyclopedias. However, the mind-boggling number of Internet sites often makes researchers lives difficult because of the amount of information available. This is why certain companies have created search engines that facilitate and organize research. There have been numerous new areas of activity, among these search-engine optimization and home-page optimization.

It wasn't very long ago that media suppliers decided the content and timing of available information, advertising and entertainment. Twenty-first century consumers have greater control and can decide for themselves what and when they want to watch or listen to something. Prominent media companies have had to adapt to the Internet.

The advent of smartphones, portable media players and wireless Internet connection all allow consumers to watch and listen to shows, news, and movies when and where they want.

This LES is related to sections 1.1 to 1.3.

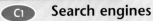

Search engines

Search-engine optimization involves the creation of programs that classify Web sites as a function of the Web user's criteria. The Web site that appears at the top of the search results should be the most relevant. Below is a sample ranking algorithm used by a search engine:

Ranking algorithm for a Web site according to user's key word

Variables taken into account

Percentage i of Web users who, after a search based on one key word, consulted the resulting site and stayed for more than 1 min.	Percentage a of the appearance of the key word in the resulting site.

Web site filters

The only Web sites that will be considered have the following:

- The percentage a of the appearance of the key word is greater than 1% and less than 10%.
- The percentage i of Web users is greater than 2%.
- The ratio $\frac{i}{a}$ is greater than 0.5 and the ratio $\frac{a}{i}$ is greater than $\frac{1}{8}$.

Ranking of filtered Web sites

- Each 1% of Web users gives 99 points, and each 1% appearance of the key word gives 70 points.
- The ranking position is obtained by subtracting 10 000 from the total number of points and by rounding the result to the next whole number.

Below are characteristics of two Web sites for a search resulting from the key word "printer."

		Site A	Site B
Number of Web users who performed this search		143 278	
Number of Web users who consulted this site and stayed	less than one minute	45 280	46 512
	more than one minute	15 093	3 488
Number of words on this site		21 346	43 739
Number of times the key word appeared		527	2 292

Do the following:

- If the Web site is not filtered, calculate the percentage of the appearance of the key word that would allow this site to be filtered.
- If the Web site has already been filtered, determine the percentage of the appearance of the key word that would result in an improvement of at least 200 places in this site's ranking.

This LES is related to section 1.4.

LES 2

C2

The home page

A home page is usually the entrance to an Internet site. Optimization of these pages consists of maximizing their efficiency and their look in order to entice users to visit a Web site for as long as possible.

Certain factors such as the quantity of text, the number of graphics and sound effects on a home page influence Web users' perception of the site. Following are survey results from Web users about the characteristics of an acceptable home page:

- The page's loading time should not be greater than 20 s.

- The page should contain between 100 to 600 words.

- A maximum of 75% of the page should contain graphics.

- Each graphic should, on average, occupy 1.5% of the home page's surface.

- The home page should contain at least one graphic element for every 40 words.

According to various Internet specialists, the following is true:

- The mean loading time for one word is 0.02 s.

- The mean loading time for a graphic is 0.2 s.

- The number N of Web users that visit a site and the mean time T (in s) of a visit vary according to the rules $N = 15x + 35y - 100t$ and $T = 60 - 2t + 0.1(x + y)$ where x is the number of words, y is the number of graphics and t is the loading time (in s) of the home page.

- The profits resulting from a site that sells music are proportional to the total visit time on the site which corresponds to the expression $N \times T$.

The designer of a home page for a site that sells music must choose between two objectives.

Objective **1**	Objective **2**
Maximize a Web user's visit time.	Maximize the number of visits.

Determine which of these two objectives is more financially advantageous and provide the characteristics of the home page that will allow for this objective.

LES 3

C3 **The best medium**

The managers of an electronics store have hired a marketing consultant to help optimize their investments in publicity. Following is a discussion between the consultant and a member of the store's management:

HOW DO YOU ADVERTISE YOUR PRODUCTS?

WE PUT ADS IN NEWSPAPERS AND WE POST ADVERTISING ON OUR WEBSITE.

WHICH MEDIUM IS THE MOST EFFECTIVE?

IT'S HARD TO SAY. IT'S TRUE THAT WE REACH MORE PEOPLE BY INTERNET THAN THROUGH NEWSPAPERS. HOWEVER, OUR STUDIES SHOW THAT ONLY 1.2% OF PEOPLE CONTACTED THROUGH THE INTERNET BECOME CLIENTS COMPARED TO 3.4% OF THOSE CONTACTED THROUGH NEWSPAPERS.

ARE THERE ANY RESTRICTIONS IN SELECTING THE MEDIA YOU WANT TO USE?

AT LEAST 20% OF OUR PUBLICITY BUDGET MUST BE FOR NEWSPAPERS.

WHAT IS YOUR PUBLICITY BUDGET?

OUR MONTHLY BUDGET IS AT LEAST $5,000 AND AT MOST $7,000. OUR STUDIES SHOW THAT EACH DOLLAR INVESTED IN INTERNET ADVERTISING ALLOWS US TO REACH 100 PEOPLE, AND EACH DOLLAR INVESTED IN NEWSPAPER ADVERTISING ALLOWS US TO REACH AN AVERAGE OF 25 PEOPLE.

HOW MANY PEOPLE DO YOU REACH MONTHLY?

I DON'T KNOW EXACTLY. HOWEVER, TO STAY COMPETITIVE, WE HAVE TO REACH AT LEAST 250 000 EVERY MONTH.

UP TO NOW, HOW HAVE YOU DIVIDED UP YOUR ADVERTISING BUDGET?

SINCE THE INTERNET REACHES MORE PEOPLE, BUT NEWSPAPERS HAVE A GREATER EFFICIENCY RATE, WE HAVE DIVIDED OUR MONTHLY BUDGET INTO TWO EQUAL PARTS, $3,500 FOR THE INTERNET AND $3,500 FOR NEWSPAPERS.

Produce a report for the store managers. This report should include the following:

- An explanation as to why their current method of budgeting their advertising is not the best way.
- A proposal for the best strategy for investing in advertising.
- The steps and calculations on which you base your explanations.

Industrial efficiency

Learning context

Companies focus on the optimal use of production time and materials involved in making or wrapping products. Whether a company is automating an assembly line or designing an item, producing efficiently and reducing the materials used are among the managers' main focuses.

Even if the time and materials required to produce a single item are minimal, they are multiplied thousands and even millions of times over when the items are produced on a large scale. This can lead to significant financial losses, wasted materials and, consequently, environmental degradation.

Optimal packaging must therefore be designed in order to properly protect the goods that are wrapped and bring them to the attention of the consumer while using as little material as possible to avoid over-packaging.

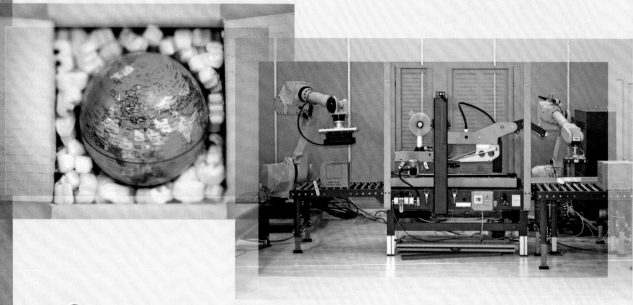

This LES is related
to sections 2.1 and 2.2.

LES 4

C2

The robotic arm

In order to speed up certain steps on a production line, many industries make use of robots. These robots can continuously and precisely perform tasks that would take considerably more time if they were carried out by humans.

The robots are moved by servomotors that are controlled by electronic chips, and these chips store instructions that resemble rules for geometric transformations.

The robotic arm shown in the graph below has the following characteristics:

- Servomotor **1** located at the origin of the plane controls the arm's rotation. The angle of rotation corresponds to a multiple of 90°.

- Servomotor **2** located between the origin and the head controls the arm's extension and retraction.

- The head includes a machine that welds with great precision.

- At its initial position, the head is located at coordinates (-8, -4).

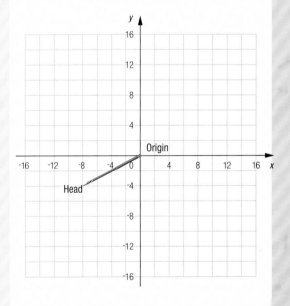

The robotic arm must weld at points A(-4, -2), B(-4, 8), C(16, 8), D(8, 4) and E(4, -8) and then return to its initial position before starting over.

A trainee claims that to minimize the distance travelled by the head of the robotic arm, the following order for the welding is the most efficient: points A, B, C, D and E then returning to the base.

Electronic chips have been miniaturized to such a degree that they are now produced by extremely precise industrial robots.

Your task consists of the following:

- Verify whether the claim made by the trainee is true or false.

- Use rules of geometric transformations to define instructions that allow the robotic arm to complete all the welding efficiently then return to the base.

161

This LES is related
to sections 2.3 and 2.4.

○ LES 5

C1

A perfect tent

Since prehistoric times, humans have used tents as dwellings that are more or less temporary and mobile. While prehistoric tents were covered with animal skins, modern tents are made of canvas or synthetic fibres, depending on their intended use. For instance, tents can be used for recreational camping, military camps or emergency shelters during humanitarian crises.

A yurt is a traditional tent covered with skins or felt patches used by the nomadic peoples of Central Asia. This family tent, made up of a single room, can easily be taken apart and put back together in a few hours.

Generally, recreational tents that are carried in a backpack or in a bicycle saddlebag are compact and light; on the other hand, tents that are meant to be transported in a vehicle are often bulkier and heavier.

There are many tent formats, from bivouac sacks for one person to circus big tops that can accommodate thousands of people.

Some tents, such as those used on expeditions in the Far North, are designed to withstand winds of over 100 km/h.

Your task is to design a tent based on the following criteria:
- The tent must take on the shape of a polyhedron wherein each edge corresponds to a rigid pole.
- The longest diagonal on the tent floor must measure at least 2.1 m.
- The area of the floor must be at least 3.4 m².
- The highest point inside the tent must be at least 1.2 m from the ground.

Your design must maximize the tent's living space and minimize its mass, and you must consider the following:
- The mass of 1 dm² of floor canvas is 1.5 g.
- The mass of 1 dm² of canvas used for the walls and roof is 1 g.
- The mass of 1 cm of a rigid pole is 0.7 g.

This LES is related
to sections 2.3 and 2.4.

○ LES 6

C3 **The war on over-packaging**

Even though packaging products is a necessity, the fact remains that the costs related to packaging are considerable. Once used, many un-recycled packages end up in landfill sites, contributing to problems linked to pollution.

A juice producer is looking to create a new container for fruit juice. The following considerations must be taken into account:

- The container must have a capacity of 1.25 L.
- The perimeter of the container's base must not exceed 20 cm.
- A single cubic crate must be able to pack 144 of the containers with as little unused space as possible.

Your task is to produce an advertising leaflet aimed at juice producers. This leaflet should state the merits of your proposed packaging format with regard to saving material and space.

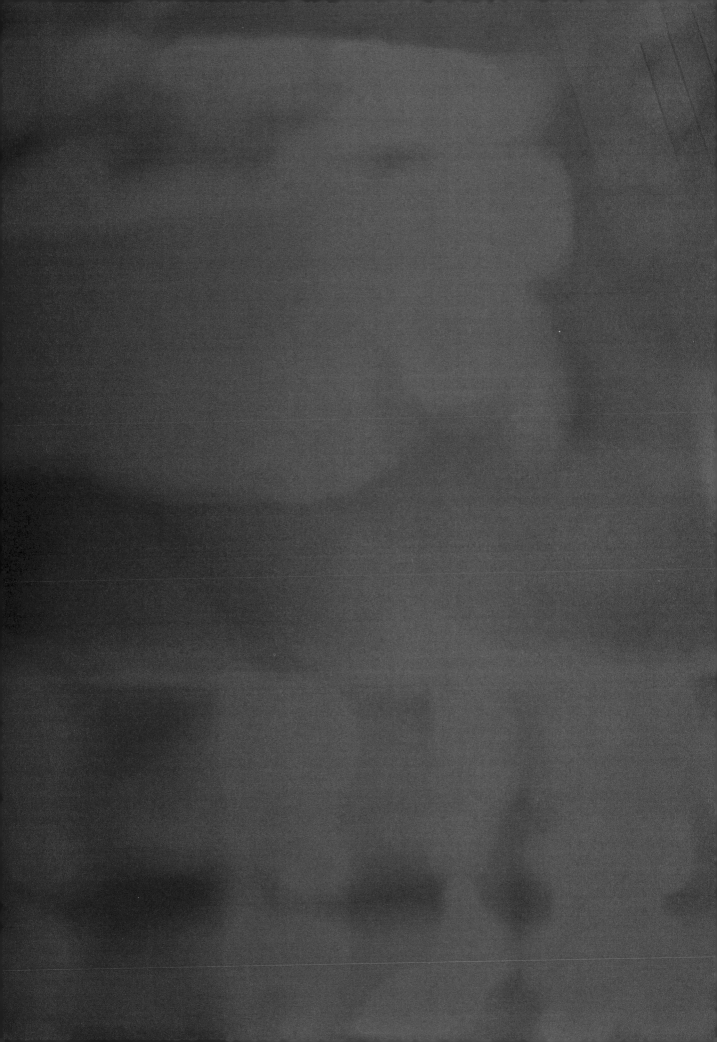

REFERENC
TABLE OF CONTENTS

Graphing calculator

Sample calculations

It is possible to perform scientific calculations and to evaluate both algebraic and logical expressions.

Graphing keys

Display screen

Cursor keys

Editing keys

Menu keys

Scientific calculation keys

Scientific calculations

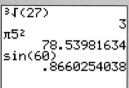

Logical expressions

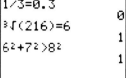

Algebraic expressions

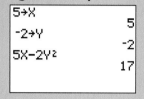

Probability

1. Display the probability menu.

- Among other things, this menu allows the simulation of random experiments. The fifth option generates a series of random whole numbers. Syntax: `randInt` (minimum value, maximum value, number of repetitions).

2 Display calculations and results.

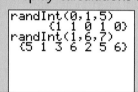

- The first example simulates flipping a coin 5 times where 0 represents tails and 1 represents heads. The second example simulates seven rolls of a die with 6 faces.

Display a table of values

1. Define the rules.

- This screen allows you to enter and edit the rules for one or more functions where Y is the dependent variable and X is the independent variable.

2. Define the viewing window.

- This screen allows you to define the viewing window for a table of values in Y indicating the starting value of X and the step size for the variation of X.

3. Display the table.

X	Y₁	Y₂
0	1	0
1	2	.5
2	4	2
3	8	4.5
4	16	8
5	32	12.5
6	64	18

X=0

- This screen allows you to display the table of values of the rules defined.

Display a graphical representation

1. Define the rules.

- If desired, the thickness of the curve (normal, thick or dotted) can be adjusted for each rule.

2. Define the viewing window.

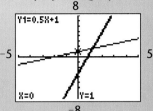

- This screen allows you to define the viewing window by limiting the Cartesian plane: $Xscl$ and $Yscl$ correspond to the step value on the respective axes.

3. Display the graph.

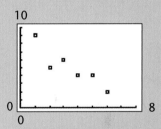

- This screen allows you to display the graphical representation of the rules previously defined. If desired, the cursor can be moved along the curves and the coordinates displayed.

Display a scatter plot and statistical calculations

1. Enter the data.

- This screen allows you to enter the data from a distribution. For a two-variable distribution, data entry is done in two columns.

2. Select the mode of representation.

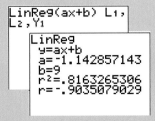

- This screen allows you to choose the type of statistical diagram.

  ⊡ : scatter plot

  ⬈ : broken-line graph

  📊 : histogram

  ⊡ : box and whisker plot

3. Display the diagram.

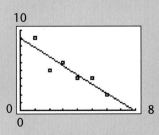

- This screen allows you to display the scatter plot.

4. Perform statistical calculations.

```
EDIT CALC TESTS
1:1-Var Stats
2:2-Var Stats
3:Med-Med
4:LinReg(ax+b)
5:QuadReg
6:CubicReg
7↓QuartReg
```

- This menu allows you to access different statistical calculations, in particular that of the linear regression.

5. Determine the regression and correlation.

```
LinReg(ax+b) L1,
L2,Y1
LinReg
y=ax+b
a=-1.142857143
b=9
r²=.8163265306
r=-.9035079029
```

- These screens allow you to obtain the equation of the regression line and the value of the correlation coefficient.

6. Display the line.

- The regression line can be displayed on the scatter plot.

Spreadsheet

A spreadsheet is software that allows you to perform calculations on numbers entered into cells. It is used mainly to perform calculations on large amounts of data, to construct tables and to draw graphs.

Spreadsheet interface

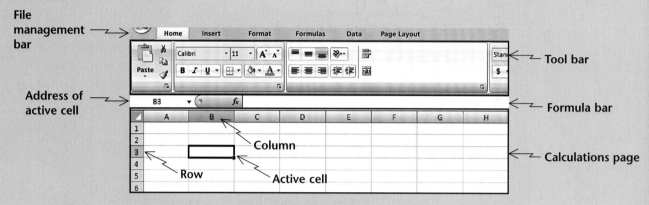

What is a cell?

A cell is the intersection of a column and a row. A column is identified by a letter and a row is identified by a number. Thus, the first cell in the upper right hand corner is identified as A1.

Entry of numbers, text and formulas in the cells

You can enter a number, text or a formula in a cell after clicking on it. Formulas allow you to perform calculations on numbers already entered in the cells. To enter a formula in a cell, just select it and begin by entering the "=" symbol.

E.g.
Column **A** contains the data to be used in the calculations.

In the spreadsheet, certain functions are predefined to calculate the sum, the minimum, the maximum, the mode, the median, the mean and the mean deviation of a set of data.

◇	A	B	C	
1	Results			
2	27.4	Number of data	17	→ =COUNT(A2:A18)
3	30.15			
4	15	Sum	527	→ =SUM(A2:A18)
5	33.8			
6	12.3	Minimum	12.3	→ =MIN(A2:A18)
7	52.6			
8	28.75	Maximum	52.6	→ =MAX(A2:A18)
9	38.25			
10	21.8	Mode	33.8	→ =MODE(A2:A18)
11	35			
12	29.5	Median	30.15	→ =MEDIAN(A2:A18)
13	27.55			
14	33.8	Average	31	→ =AVERAGE(A2:A18)
15	15			
16	33.8	Mean deviation	8.417647059	→ =MEAN DEVIATION (A2:A18) or =C4/C2
17	50			
18	42.3			
19				

How to construct a graph

Below is a procedure for drawing a graph using a spreadsheet.

1) Select the range of data.

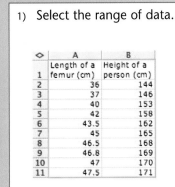

	A	B
	Length of a femur (cm)	Height of a person (cm)
1		
2	36	144
3	37	146
4	40	153
5	42	158
6	43.5	162
7	45	165
8	46.5	168
9	46.8	169
10	47	170
11	47.5	171

2) Select from the graph assistant.

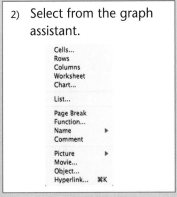

3) Choose the graph type.

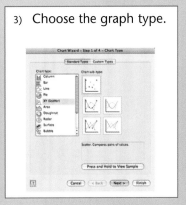

4) Confirm the data for the graph.

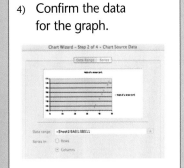

5) Choose graph options.

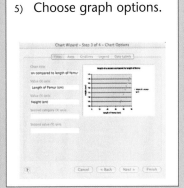

6) Choose the location of the graph.

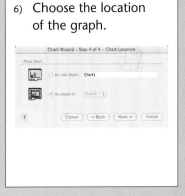

7) Draw the graph.

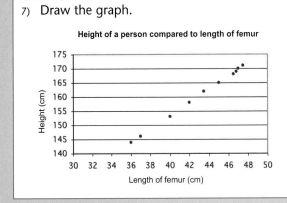

After drawing the graph, you can modify different elements by double-clicking on the element to be changed: title, scale, legend, grid, type of graph, etc.

Below are different types of graphs you can create using a spreadsheet:

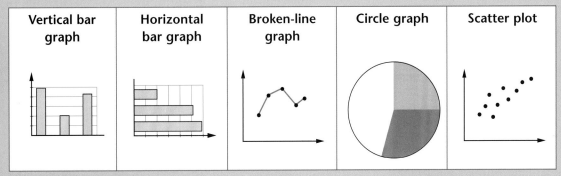

Vertical bar graph	Horizontal bar graph	Broken-line graph	Circle graph	Scatter plot

Dynamic geometry software

Dynamic geometry software allows you to draw and move objects in a workspace. The dynamic aspect of this type of software allows you to explore and verify geometric properties and to validate constructions.

The workspace and the tools

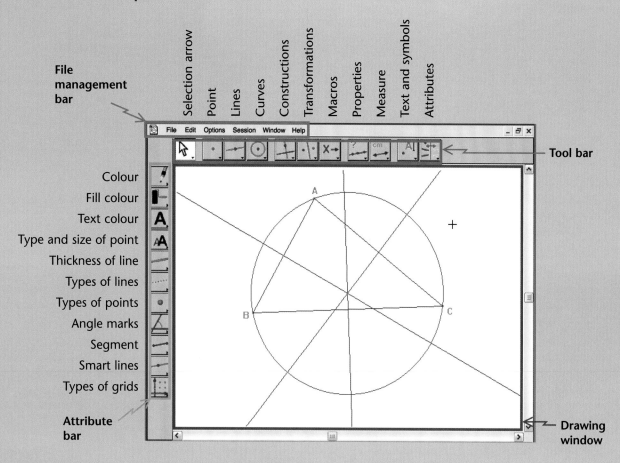

Cursors and their interpretations

$+$	Cursor used when moving in the drawing window.
✋	Cursor used when drawing an object.
What object?	Cursor used when there are several objects.
☟	Cursor used when tracing an object.
✍	Cursor used to indicate movement of an object is possible.
↖	Cursor used when working in the file management bar and in the tool bar.
🖌	Cursor used when filling an object with a colour.
✎	Cursor used to change the attribute of the selected object.

Geometric explorations

1) A median separates a triangle into two other triangles. In order to explore the properties of these two triangles, perform the following construction. To verify that triangles ABD and ACD have the same area, calculate the area of each triangle. By moving the points A, B and C, notice that the areas of the two triangles are always the same.

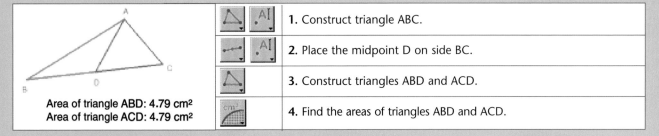

	1. Construct triangle ABC.
	2. Place the midpoint D on side BC.
	3. Construct triangles ABD and ACD.
	4. Find the areas of triangles ABD and ACD.

Area of triangle ABD: 4.79 cm²
Area of triangle ACD: 4.79 cm²

2) In order to determine the relation between the position of the midpoint of the hypotenuse in a right triangle and the three vertices of the triangle, perform the construction below. By moving points A, B, and C, note that the midpoint of the hypotenuse of a right triangle is equidistant from its three vertices.

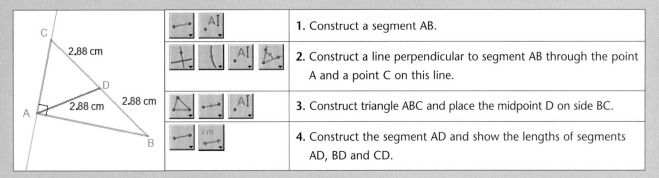

	1. Construct a segment AB.
	2. Construct a line perpendicular to segment AB through the point A and a point C on this line.
	3. Construct triangle ABC and place the midpoint D on side BC.
	4. Construct the segment AD and show the lengths of segments AD, BD and CD.

Graphical exploration

In order to discover the relation between the slopes of two perpendicular lines in the Cartesian plane, perform the construction below. By showing the product of the slopes and modifying the inclination of one of the lines, note a particular property of these slopes: the product of the slopes of these two perpendicular lines is -1.

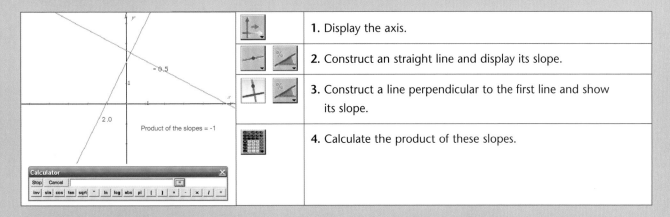

	1. Display the axis.
	2. Construct an straight line and display its slope.
	3. Construct a line perpendicular to the first line and show its slope.
	4. Calculate the product of these slopes.

Notations and symbols

Notation & symbols	Meaning
{ }	Brace brackets, used to identify the elements in a set
$\mathbb{N}$	The set of Natural numbers
$\mathbb{Z}$	The set of Integers
$\mathbb{Q}$	The set of Rational numbers
$\mathbb{Q}'$	The set of Irrational numbers
$\mathbb{R}$	The set of Real numbers
$\cup$	The union of sets
$\cap$	The intersection of sets
Ω	Read "omega," it represents the sample space in a random experiment
$\varnothing$ or { }	The empty set (or null set)
=	… is equal to…
$\neq$	… is not equal to… or …is different than…
$\approx$	… is approximately equal to…
<	… is less than…
>	… is greater than…
$\leq$	… is less than or equal to…
$\geq$	… is greater than or equal to…
$[a, b]$	Interval, including a and b
$[a, b[$	Interval, including a but excluding b
$]a, b]$	Interval, excluding a but including b
$]a, b[$	Interval, excluding a and b
∞	Infinity
(a, b)	The ordered pair a and b
$f(x)$	Read "f of x," the value (image) of the function f at x
f^{-1}	The inverse of function f
$f \circ g$	Read "f of g," composite of function g followed by function f
( )	Parentheses show which operation to perform first
$-a$	The opposite of a

Notation & symbol	Meaning
$\frac{1}{a}$ or a^{-1}	The reciprocal of a
a^2	The second power of a or a squared
a^3	The third power of a or a cubed
$\sqrt[3]{a}$	The cube root of a
$\sqrt{a}$	The square root of a
$|a|$	The absolute value of a
%	Percentage
$a:b$	The ratio of a to b
π	Read "pi," it is approximately equal to 3.1416
$\overline{AB}$	Segment AB
m $\overline{AB}$	Measure of segment AB
$\angle$	Angle
m $\angle$	Measure of an angle
$\overset{\frown}{AB}$	Arc AB
m $\overset{\frown}{AB}$	The measure of arc AB
//	... is parallel to...
$\perp$	... is perpendicular to...
⌐	Indicates a right angle in a plane figure
$\triangle$	Triangle
$\cong$	... is congruent to...
~	... is similar to...
$\hat{=}$	... corresponds to...
$P(E)$	Probability of event E
$P(A \mid B)$	Probability that event B will occur given that event A has already occurred
A'	Read "complement," it is the complementary event to event A
Med	The median of a distribution
Q_1, Q_2, Q_3	First, second and third quartiles of a distribution
Δx	Read "delta," it is the variation or growth in x

Notation & symbol	Meaning
d(A, B)	Distance between points A and B
°	Degree
rad	Radian
sin A	Sine of angle A
cos A	Cosine of angle A
tan A	Tangent of angle A
arcsin x	Arcsin of angle x
arccos x	Arccos of angle x
arctan x	Arctan of angle x
sec A	Secant of angle A
cosec A	Cosec of angle A
cotan A	Cotan of angle A
$[a]$	Integer part of a
$\log_c a$	Logarithm of a in base c
$\log a$	Logarithm of a in base 10
$\ln a$	Logarithm of a in base e
$a!$	Factorial of a
t	Translation
r	Rotation
s	Reflection
h	Dilatation
$\vec{a}$	Vector a
$\|\vec{a}\|$	Norm of vector a
$\vec{a} \cdot \vec{b}$	Scalar product of vector a and vector b

International system of units (SI)

Base units

Measure	Unit	Symbol
length	metre	m
mass	kilogram	kg
time, duration	second	s
electric current	ampere	A
temperature	kelvin	K
amount of a substance	mole	mol
luminous intensity	candela	cd

Acceptable units for SI

Measure	Unit	Symbol
area or surface area	square metre hectare	m^2 ha
angle	degree	°
electric potential difference	volt	V
energy, work	joule watt hour	J Wh
force	newton	N
frequency	hertz	H
mass	ton	t
pressure	pascal millimetre of mercury	Pa mmHg
energy	watt	W
electrical resistance	ohm	Ω
temperature	degree Celsius	°C
time	minute hour day	min h d
speed	metre per second kilometre per hour	m/s km/h
volume	cubic metre litre	m^3 L

Prefixes for SI

Multiplicative factor	Name	Symbol	Multiplicative factor	Name	Symbol
10^1	deca	da	10^{-1}	deci	d
10^2	hecto	h	10^{-2}	centi	c
10^3	kilo	k	10^{-3}	milli	m
10^6	mega	M	10^{-6}	micro	μ
10^9	giga	G	10^{-9}	nano	n

Geometric statements

	Statement	Example
1.	If two lines are parallel to a third line, then they are all parallel to each other.	If $l_1 \parallel l_2$ and $l_2 \parallel l_3$, then $l_1 \parallel l_3$.
2.	If two lines are perpendicular to a third line, then the two lines are parallel to each other.	If $l_1 \perp l_3$ and $l_2 \perp l_3$, then $l_1 \parallel l_2$.
3.	If two lines are parallel, then every line perpendicular to one of these lines is perpendicular to the other.	If $l_1 \parallel l_2$ and $l_3 \perp l_2$, then $l_3 \perp l_1$.
4.	If the exterior arms of two adjacent angles are collinear, then the angles are supplementary.	The points A, B and D are collinear. $\angle$ ABC & $\angle$ CBD are adjacent and supplementary.
5.	If the exterior arms of two adjacent angles are perpendicular, then the angles are complementary.	$\overline{AB} \perp \overline{BD}$ $\angle$ ABC and $\angle$ CBD are adjacent and complementary.
6.	Vertically opposite angles are congruent.	$\angle 1 \cong \angle 3$ $\angle 2 \cong \angle 4$
7.	If a transversal intersects two parallel lines, then the alternate interior, alternate exterior and corresponding angles are respectively congruent.	If $l_1 \parallel l_2$, then angles 1, 3, 5 and 7 are congruent as are angles 2, 4, 6 and 8.
8.	If a transversal intersects two lines resulting in congruent corresponding angles (or alternate interior angles or alternate exterior angles), then those two lines are parallel.	In the figure for statement 7, if the angles 1, 3, 5 and 7 are congruent and the angles 2, 4, 6 and 8 are congruent, then $l_1 \parallel l_2$.
9.	If a transversal intersects two parallel lines, then the interior angles on the same side of the transversal are supplementary.	If $l_1 \parallel l_2$, then $m \angle 1 + m \angle 2 = 180°$ and $m \angle 3 + m \angle 4 = 180°$.

	Statement	Example
10.	The sum of the measures of the interior angles of a triangle is 180°.	$m \angle 1 + m \angle 2 + m \angle 3 = 180°$
11.	Corresponding elements of congruent plane or solid figures have the same measurements.	$\overline{AD} \cong \overline{A'D'}$, $\overline{CD} \cong \overline{C'D'}$, $\overline{BC} \cong \overline{B'C'}$, $\overline{AB} \cong \overline{A'B'}$ $\angle A \cong \angle A'$, $\angle B \cong \angle B'$, $\angle C \cong \angle C'$, $\angle D \cong \angle D'$
12.	In an isosceles triangle, the angles opposite the congruent sides are congruent.	In the isosceles triangle ABC: $\overline{AB} \cong \overline{AC}$ $\angle C \cong \angle B$
13.	The axis of symmetry of an isosceles triangle represents a median, a perpendicular bisector, an angle bisector and an altitude of the triangle.	Axis of symmetry of triangle ABC, Median from point A Perpendicular bisector of the side BC Bisector of angle A Altitude of the triangle
14.	The opposite sides of a parallelogram are congruent.	In the parallelogram ABCD: $\overline{AB} \cong \overline{DC}$ and $\overline{AD} \cong \overline{BC}$
15.	The diagonals of a parallelogram bisect each other.	In the parallelogram ABCD: $\overline{AE} \cong \overline{EC}$ and $\overline{DE} \cong \overline{EB}$
16.	The opposite angles of a parallelogram are congruent.	In the parallelogram ABCD: $\angle A \cong \angle C$ and $\angle B \cong \angle D$
17.	In a parallelogram, the sum of the measures of two consecutive angles is 180°.	In the parallelogram ABCD: $m \angle 1 + m \angle 2 = 180°$ $m \angle 2 + m \angle 3 = 180°$ $m \angle 3 + m \angle 4 = 180°$ $m \angle 4 + m \angle 1 = 180°$
18.	The diagonals of a rectangle are congruent.	In the rectangle ABCD: $\overline{AC} \cong \overline{BD}$
19.	The diagonals of a rhombus are perpendicular.	In the rhombus ABCD: $\overline{AC} \perp \overline{BD}$
20.	The measure of an exterior angle of a triangle is equal to the sum of the measures of the interior angles at the other two vertices.	$m \angle 3 = m \angle 1 + m \angle 2$

	Statement	Example
21.	In a triangle the longest side is opposite the largest angle.	In triangle ABC, the largest angle is A, therefore the longest side is BC.
22.	In a triangle, the smallest angle is opposite the smallest side.	In triangle ABC, the smallest angle is B, therefore the smallest side is AC.
23.	The sum of the measures of two sides in a triangle is larger than the measure of the third side.	$2 + 5 > 4$ $2 + 4 > 5$ $4 + 5 > 2$ 5 cm 2 cm 4 cm
24.	The sum of the measures of the interior angles of a quadrilateral is 360°.	$m \angle 1 + m \angle 2 + m \angle 3 + m \angle 4 = 360°$
25.	The sum of the measures of the interior angles of a polygon with n sides is $n \times 180° - 360°$ or $(n - 2) \times 180°$.	$n \times 180° - 360°$ or $(n - 2) \times 180°$
26.	The sum of the measures of the exterior angles (one at each vertex) of a convex polygon is 360°.	$m \angle 1 + m \angle 2 + m \angle 3 +$ $m \angle 4 + m \angle 5 + m \angle 6 = 360°$
27.	The corresponding angles of similar plane figures or of similar solids are congruent and the measures of the corresponding sides are proportional.	The triangle ABC is similar to triangle A'B'C': $\angle A \cong \angle A'$ $\angle B \cong \angle B'$ $\angle C \cong \angle C'$ $\dfrac{m\ \overline{A'B'}}{m\ \overline{AB}} = \dfrac{m\ \overline{B'C'}}{m\ \overline{BC}} = \dfrac{m\ \overline{A'C'}}{m\ \overline{AC}}$
28.	In similar plane figures, the ratio of the areas is equal to the square of the ratio of similarity.	In the above figures, $\dfrac{m\ \overline{A'B'}}{m\ \overline{AB}} = \dfrac{m\ \overline{B'C'}}{m\ \overline{BC}} = \dfrac{m\ \overline{A'C'}}{m\ \overline{AC}} = k$ ← Ratio of similarity $\dfrac{\text{area of triangle A'B'C'}}{\text{area of triangle ABC}} = k^2$
29.	Three non-collinear points define one and only one circle.	There is only one circle which contains the points A, B and C.
30.	The perpendicular bisectors of any chords in a circle intersect at the centre of the circle.	l_1 and l_2 are the perpendicular bisectors of the chords AB and CD. The point of intersection M of these perpendicular bisectors is the centre of the circle.

	Statement	Example
31.	All the diameters of a circle are congruent.	$\overline{AD}$, $\overline{BE}$ and $\overline{CF}$ are diameters of the circle with centre O. $\overline{AD} \cong \overline{BE} \cong \overline{CF}$
32.	In a circle, the length of the radius is one-half the length of the diameter.	$\overline{AB}$ is a diameter of the circle with centre O. $m\,\overline{OA} = \frac{1}{2}\,m\,\overline{AB}$
33.	In a circle, the ratio of the circumference to the diameter is a constant represented by π.	$\frac{C}{d} = \pi$
34.	In a circle, a central angle has the same degree measure as the arc contained between its sides.	In the circle with centre O, $m \angle AOB = m\,\widehat{AB}$ stated in degrees.
35.	In a circle, the ratio of the measures of two central angles is equal to the ratio of the arcs intercepted by their sides.	$\dfrac{m \angle AOB}{m \angle COD} = \dfrac{m\,\widehat{AB}}{m\,\widehat{CD}}$
36.	In a circle, the ratio of the areas of two sectors is equal to the ratio of the measures of the angles at the centre of these sectors.	$\dfrac{\text{Area of the sector AOB}}{\text{Area of the sector COD}} = \dfrac{m \angle AOB}{m \angle COD}$
37.	In a right triangle, the square of the length of the hypotenuse is equal to the sum of the squares of the lengths of the legs.	$\left(m\,\overline{AB}\right)^2 = \left(m\,\overline{AC}\right)^2 + \left(m\,\overline{BC}\right)^2$
38.	Two triangles whose corresponding sides are congruent are congruent (SSS).	$\overline{AB} \cong \overline{DE}$, $\overline{BC} \cong \overline{EF}$, $\overline{AC} \cong \overline{DF}$ Therefore $\triangle ABC \cong \triangle DEF$.
39.	Two triangles that have a congruent side contained between corresponding congruent angles are congruent (ASA).	$\angle A \cong \angle D$, $\overline{AB} \cong \overline{DE}$, $\angle B \cong \angle E$ Therefore $\triangle ABC \cong \triangle DEF$.

Statement	Example
40. Two triangles that have a congruent angle contained between corresponding congruent sides are congruent (SAS).	$\overline{AB} \cong \overline{DE}$, $\angle A \cong \angle D$, $\overline{AC} \cong \overline{DF}$ Therefore $\triangle ABC \cong \triangle DEF$.
41. Two triangles that have two corresponding congruent angles are similar (AA).	$\angle A \cong \angle D$, $\angle B \cong \angle E$ Therefore $\triangle ABC \sim \triangle DEF$.
42. Two triangles that have a congruent angle contained between corresponding sides of proportional length are similar (SAS).	$\dfrac{m\,\overline{AB}}{m\,\overline{DE}} = \dfrac{m\,\overline{AC}}{m\,\overline{DF}}$ and $\angle A \cong \angle D$. Therefore $\triangle ABC \sim \triangle DEF$.
43. Two triangles that have three sides of proportional length are similar (SSS).	$\dfrac{m\,\overline{AB}}{m\,\overline{DE}} = \dfrac{m\,\overline{AC}}{m\,\overline{DF}} = \dfrac{m\,\overline{BC}}{m\,\overline{EF}}$ Therefore $\triangle ABC \sim \triangle DEF$.
44. Transversals intersecting parallel lines are divided into segments of proportional lengths.	$\dfrac{m\,\overline{AB}}{m\,\overline{FE}} = \dfrac{m\,\overline{BC}}{m\,\overline{ED}}$

	Statement	Example
45.	In a right triangle, the length of a leg of a right triangle is the geometric mean of the length of its projection on the hypotenuse and the length of the hypotenuse.	$$\frac{m\,\overline{AD}}{m\,\overline{AB}} = \frac{m\,\overline{AB}}{m\,\overline{AC}} \text{ or } \left(m\,\overline{AB}\right)^2 = m\,\overline{AD} \times m\,\overline{AC}$$ $$\frac{m\,\overline{CD}}{m\,\overline{BC}} = \frac{m\,\overline{BC}}{m\,\overline{AC}} \text{ or } \left(m\,\overline{BC}\right)^2 = m\,\overline{CD} \times m\,\overline{AC}$$
46.	In a right triangle, the length of the altitude drawn from the right angle is the geometric mean of the length of the two segments that determine the hypotenuse.	$$\frac{m\,\overline{AD}}{m\,\overline{BD}} = \frac{m\,\overline{BD}}{m\,\overline{CD}} \text{ or } \left(m\,\overline{BD}\right)^2 = m\,\overline{AD} \times m\,\overline{CD}$$
47.	In a right triangle, the product of the length of the hypotenuse and its corresponding altitude is equal to the product of the length of the legs.	$$m\,\overline{AC} \times m\,\overline{BD} = m\,\overline{AB} \times m\,\overline{BC}$$
48.	In a right triangle, the length of the side that is opposite to a 30° angle is equal to half the length of the hypotenuse.	$$m\,\overline{AC} = \frac{m\,\overline{AB}}{2}$$
49.	The length of the sides of a triangle are proportional to the sine of the angles that are opposite to them.	$$\frac{a}{\sin A} = \frac{b}{\sin B} = \frac{c}{\sin C}$$

Glossary

A

Angles

Classification of angles according to their measure

Name	Measure	Representation
Zero	0°	
Acute	Between 0° and 90°	
Right	90°	
Obtuse	Between 90° and 180°	
Straight	180°	
Reflex	Between 180° and 360°	
Perigon	360°	

Angles
Alternate exterior, p. 176
Alternate interior, p. 176
Corresponding, p. 176

Apothem of a regular polygon
Segment (or length of segment) from the centre of the regular polygon perpendicular to any of its sides. It is determined by the centre of the regular polygon and the midpoint of any side.
E.g.

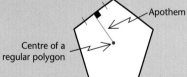

Apothem
Centre of a regular polygon

Arccosine
Operation that allows you to calculate the measure of an angle based on the value of cosine of this angle. Arccosine can also be written as $\cos^{-1}$.

Arc of a circle
Portion of the circle defined by two points.

Arcsine
Operation that allows you to calculate the measure of an angle based on value of the sine of this angle. Arcsine can also be written as $\sin^{-1}$.

Arctangent
Operation that allows you to calculate the measure of an angle based on value of the tangent of this angle. Arctangent can also be written as $\tan^{-1}$.

Area
The measure of the surface of a figure. Area is expressed in square units.

Area of a circle, p. 84

Area of a parallelogram, p. 84

Area of a rectangle, p. 84

Area of a regular polygon, p. 84

Area of a rhombus, p. 84

Area of a right-circular cone

$$A_{\text{right-circular cone}} = \pi r^2 + \pi ra$$

Area of a sector

$$\frac{\left(\begin{array}{c}\text{Measure of the central} \\ \text{angle of a sector}\end{array}\right)}{360°} = \frac{\text{sector area}}{\pi r^2}$$

Area of a sphere, p. 84

Area of a square, p. 84

Area of a trapezoid, p. 84

Area of a triangle, p. 84

B

Boundary line, p. 9

C

Capacity
Volume of a fluid which a solid can contain.

Cartesian plane
A plane formed by two graduated perpendicular lines.

Centre angle
Angle formed by two radii of a circle. The vertex of the angle corresponds to the centre of the circle.

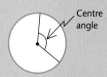

Centre angle

Change of scale, p. 107

Circle
A closed line that is made of points that are located at an equal distance from the same point called the centre.

Circle

Centre of circle

Circumference
The perimeter of a circle. In a circle whose circumference is C, the diameter is d and the radius is r: $C = \pi d$ and $C = 2\pi r$.

Coordinates of a point
Each of the two numbers used to describe the position of a point in a Cartesian plane.

Cosine of an angle
In a right triangle where A is the vertex of the acute angle:

$$\cos A = \frac{\text{length of leg adjacent to } \angle A}{\text{length of hypotenuse}}$$

Cube root
The inverse of the operation which consists of cubing a number is called finding the cube root. The symbol for this operation is $\sqrt[3]{\ }$.

E.g. 1) $\sqrt[3]{125} = 5$
       2) $\sqrt[3]{-8} = -2$

Degree of a monomial
The sum of the exponents of the monomial.
E.g. 1) The degree of the monomial 9 is 0.
      2) The degree of the monomial $-7xy$ is 2.
      3) The degree of the monomial $15a^2$ is 2.

Degree of a polynomial in one variable
The largest exponent of that variable in the polynomial.
E.g. The degree of the polynomial $7x^3 - x^2 + 4$ is 3.

Diameter
Segment or length of segment that joins two points on a circle and passes through the centre of the circle.

Diameter

Dilatation, pp. 83, 107

Distance between two points
In a Cartesian plane, the distance d between points $A(x_1, y_1)$ and $B(x_2, y_2)$ is calculated using the formula $d = \sqrt{(x_2 - x_1)^2 + (y_2 - y_1)^2}$.

Edge
Segment formed by the intersection of any two faces of a solid.

Equation
Mathematical statement of equality involving one or more variables.
E.g. $4x - 8 = 4$

Equivalent equations
Equations having the same solution.
E.g. $2x = 10$ and $3x = 15$ are equivalent equations, because the solution of each is 5.

Equivalent figures, pp. 119, 130

Equivalent lines, p. 119

Equivalent plane figures, pp. 119, 130

Equivalent solids, pp. 119, 132

Exponentiation
Operation which consists of raising a base to an exponent.
E.g. In 5^8, the base is 5 and the exponent is 8.

Face
Plane or curved surface bound by edges.

Function
A relation between two variables in which each value of the independent variable is associated with at most one value of the dependent variable.

Geometric transformation, pp. 82, 95

Half-plane, pp. 9, 10

Heron's formula
A formula that allows you to calculate the area of a triangle based on the length of the three sides of this triangle. In the adjacent triangle,

$A_{\text{triangle}} = \sqrt{p(p - a)(p - b)(p - c)}$ where p represents the half-perimeter of the triangle, which is calculated as $p = \dfrac{a + b + c}{2}$.

Height of a triangle (altitude)
Segment from one vertex of a triangle perpendicular to the line containing the opposite side.

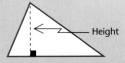

Hypotenuse
The side that is opposite the right angle in a right triangle. It is the longest side in a right triangle.

I

Inequality, pp. 8, 9, 18

Integer
A number belonging to the set $\mathbb{Z} = \{...,-2, -1, 0, 1, 2, 3, ...\}$.

Interval
A set of all the real numbers between two given numbers called the endpoints. Each endpoint can be either included or excluded in the interval.
E.g. The interval of real numbers from -2 included to 9 excluded is [-2, 9[.

Irrational number
A number which cannot be expressed as a ratio of two integers, and whose decimal representation is non-periodic and non-terminating.

Isoceles trapezoid
A trapezoid that is made up of two congruent sides.
E.g.

L

Laws of exponents

Law	
Product of powers:	$a^m \times a^n = a^{m+n}$
Quotient of powers: For $a \neq 0$	$\dfrac{a^m}{a^n} = a^{m-n}$
Power of a product:	$(ab)^m = a^m b^m$
Power of a power:	$(a^m)^n = a^{mn}$
Power of a quotient: $b \neq 0$:	$\left(\dfrac{a}{b}\right)^m = \dfrac{a^m}{b^m}$

Legs (or arms) of a right triangle
The sides that form a right angle in a right triangle.

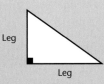

Linear programming, p. 53

M

Median of a triangle
Segment determined by a vertex and the midoint of the opposite side.
E.g. The segment AE, BF and CD are medians of triangle ABC.

Metric relations, pp. 180, 181

Monomial
Algebraic expression formed by one number, one variable or a product of numbers and variables.
E.g. 9, $-5x^2$ and $4xy$ are monomials.

N

Natural number
Any number belonging to the set

$\mathbb{N} = \{0, 1, 2, 3, ...\}$.

Optimizing function, p. 40

Origin of a Cartesian plane
The point of intersection of the two axes in a Cartesian plane. The coordinates of the origin are (0, 0).

Parallelogram
A quadrilateral that is made up of two pairs of parallel opposite sides.

E.g. $\overline{AB} \parallel \overline{DC}$
$\overline{AD} \parallel \overline{BC}$

Perimeter
The length of the boundary of a closed figure. It is expressed in units of length.

Perpendicular bisector
A perpendicular line passing through the midpoint of a segment. It is also an axis of symmetry for the segment.
E.g.

Polygon
A closed plane figure with three or more sides.

Polygons

Number of sides	Name of polygon
3	Triangle
4	Quadrilateral
5	Pentagon
6	Hexagon
7	Heptagon
8	Octagon
9	Nonagon
10	Decagon
11	Undecagon
12	Dodecagon

Polygon of constraints, p. 40

Polyhedron
A solid determined by plane polygonal faces.
E.g.

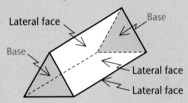

Polynomial
An algebraic expression containing one or more terms. E.g. $x^3 + 4x^2 - 18$

Prism
A polyhedron with two congruent parallel faces called "bases." The parallelograms defined by the corresponding sides of these bases are called the "lateral faces."
E.g. Triangular-based prism

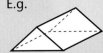

Proportion
Equality between two ratios or two rates.
E.g. 1) $3{:}11 = 12{:}44$

2) $\dfrac{7}{5} = \dfrac{14}{10}$

Pyramid
A polyhedron with one polygonal base, whose lateral faces are triangles with a common vertex called the "apex."
E.g. Octagonal-based pyramid.

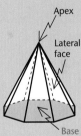

Pythagorean theorem, p. 179

Q

Quadrant
Each of the four regions determined by the axes of a Cartesian plane. The quadrants are numbered 1 to 4.

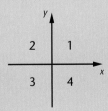

R

Radius

A radius is a segment (or length of a segment) which is determined by the centre of a circle and any point on the circle.

Radius

Rate

A way of comparing two quantities or two sizes expressed in different units and which requires division.

Ratio

A way of comparing two quantities or two sizes expressed in the same units and which requires division.

Rational number

A number which can be written as the quotient of two integers where the denominator is not zero. Its decimal representation can be terminating or non-terminating and periodic.

Ratio of similarity

Ratio of corresponding segments resulting from a dilatation.

Real number

A number belonging to the union of the set of rational numbers and the set of irrational numbers.

Rectangle

A quadrilateral that is made up of four right angles and two pairs of congruent opposite sides.
E.g.

Reflection, pp. 83, 96

Regular polygon

A polygon where all sides are congruent and all angles are congruent.

Regular prism

A prism whose bases are regular polygons.
E.g. A regular heptagonal-based prism.

Regular heptagon

Regular pyramid

A pyramid whose base is a regular polygon.
E.g. A regular hexagonal-based pyramid.

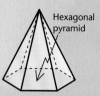

Hexagonal pyramid

Relation

A relationship between two variables.

Rhombus

A parallelogram that is made up of congruent sides.
E.g.

Right-circular cone

Solid made of two faces, a circle or a sector. The circle is the base and the sector forms the lateral face.

Right-circular cylinder

Solid made of three faces, two congruent circles and a rectangle. The circles form the bases and the rectangle forms the lateral face.

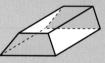

Right prism

A prism whose lateral faces are rectangles.
E.g. A right trapezoidal-based prism.

Right pyramid

A pyramid such that the segment from the apex, perpendicular to the base, intersects it at the centre of the polygonal base.
E.g. A right rectangular pyramid.

Right trapezoid

A trapezoid that is made up of two right angles.
E.g.

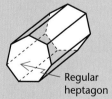

Rules for transforming equations

Rules that result in obtaining equivalent equations. Solve an equation by respecting the following:
- Adding or subtracting the same number on both sides of the equation.
- Multiplying or dividing both sides of the equation by a number other than 0.

Rules for transforming inequalities, p. 8

S

Scientific notation

A notation which facilitates the reading and writing of numbers which are very large or very small.

E.g. 1) $56\ 000\ 000 = 5.6 \times 10^7$
2) $0.000\ 000\ 008 = 8 \times 10^{-9}$

Section of a solid

The face obtained when a plane cuts a solid.
E.g.

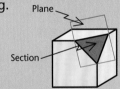

The section obtained by the intersection of this plane with this cube is a triangle.

Sector

Portion of a circle defined by two radii.

Similar figures

Two figures are similar if and only if enlargement or reduction of one results in a figure congruent to the other.

Sine law, p. 181

Sine of an angle

In a right triangle where A is the vertex of the acute angle:

$$\sin A = \frac{\text{length of leg opposite to} \angle A}{\text{length of hypotenuse}}$$

Slant height of a regular pyramid

Segment from the apex perpendicular to any side of the polygon forming the base of the pyramid. It corresponds to the altitude of a triangle which forms a lateral face.
E.g.

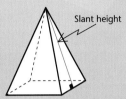

Slant height

Slant height of a right-circular cone

Segment (or length of a segment) defined by the apex and any point on edge of the base.
E.g.

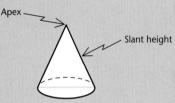

Apex

Slant height

Slope

A number that describes the inclination of a segment or a line. In a Cartesian plane, the slope **a** of a segment or a line passing through the points $A(x_1, y_1)$ and $B(x_2, y_2)$ is calculated using the formula $a = \dfrac{y_2 - y_1}{x_2 - x_1}$

Solid

Portion of space bounded by a closed surface.
E.g.

Solving a system of equations
  Comparison method, p. 7
  Elimination method, p. 7
  Graphical method, p. 7
  Substitution method, p. 7
  Table of values, p. 7

Sphere

The set of all points in space at a given distance (radius) from a given point (centre).

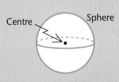

Centre

Sphere

Square
A quadrilateral that is made up of four congruent sides and four congruent angles.
E.g.

Square root
The inverse of the operation which consists of squaring a positive number is called finding the square root. The symbol for this operation is $\sqrt{}$.
E.g. The square root of 25, written $\sqrt{25}$, is 5.
   Note: $\sqrt{25}$ is called a "radical" and 25 is called the "radicand."

System of equations, p. 7

System of inequalities, p. 18

T

Tangent of an angle
In a right triangle where A is the vertex of the acute angle:

$$\tan A = \frac{\text{length of leg opposite to } \angle A}{\text{length of leg adjacent to } \angle A}$$

Terms
Algebraic term
A term can be composed of one number or of a product of numbers and variables.
E.g. 9, x and $3xy^2$ are terms.

Coefficient of a term
The number preceding the variable(s) of an algebraic term.
E.g. In the algebraic expression $x + 6xy - 4.7y$, 1, 6 and 4.7 are, respectively, the coefficients of the first, second and third terms.

Like terms
Terms composed of constant terms or the same variables raised to the same exponents.
E.g. 1) $8ax^2$ and ax^2 are like terms.
    2) 8 and 17 are like terms.

Translation, pp. 82, 95

Trapezoid
A quadrilateral that is made up of a pair of parallel sides.
E.g. AB // CD

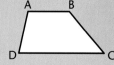

Triangle
A polygon that has three sides.

Classification of triangles

Characteristics	Name	Representation
No congruent sides	Scalene	
Two congruent sides	Isosceles	
All sides congruent	Equilateral	
Three acute angles	Acute triangle	
One obtuse angle	Obtuse triangle	
One right angle	Right triangle	
Two congruent angles	Isoangular triangle	
All angles congruent	Equiangular triangle	

Trigonometric formula
A formula that allows you to calculate the area of a triangle based on the length of two sides of this triangle and the angle contained between these two angles. In the adjacent triangle,

$$A_{\text{triangle}} = \frac{a \times b \times \sin C}{2}.$$

U

Units of area
The square metre is the basic unit of area in the metric system (SI).

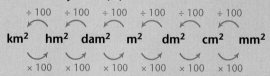

Units of capacity
The litre is the basic unit of capacity in the metric system (SI).

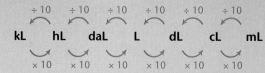

Units of length

The metre is the basic unit of length in the metric system (SI).

Units of volume

The cubic metre is the basic unit of volume in the metric system (SI).

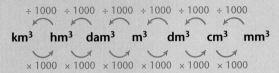

Variable

A symbol (generally a letter) which can take different values.

Vertex of a solid

In geometry, a point common to at least two edges of a solid.

Volume

A measure of the space occupied by a solid, volume is expressed in cubic units.

Volume of a right-circular cone, p. 84

Volume of a right-circular cylinder, p. 84

Volume of a right prism, p. 84

Volume of a right pyramid, p. 84

Volume of a sphere, p. 84

x-axis (horizontal)

A scaled line which allows you to determine the *x*-value (abscissa) of any point in the Cartesian plane.

x-intercept (zero)

In a Cartesian plane, an *x*-intercept is the *x*-value (abscissa) of an intersection point of a curve with the *x*-axis.

x-value (abscissa)

The first coordinate of a point in the Cartesian plane.
E.g. The *x*-value (abscissa) of the point (5, -2) is 5.

y-axis (vertical)

A scaled line which allows you to determine the *y*-value (ordinate) of any point in the Cartesian plane.

y-intercept (initial value)

In a Cartesian plane, the *y*-intercept is the *y*-value (ordinate) of an intersection point of a curve with the *y*-axis

y-value (ordinate)

The second coordinate of a point in the Cartesian plane.
E.g. The *y*-value (ordinate) of the point (5, -2) is -2.

Photography Credits

T Top   B Bottom   L Left   R Right   C Center   BG Background

Cover

(1) © Gilles Lougassi/Shutterstock

Vision 1

3 TL © Charles O'Rear/Corbis 3 TR © Radius Images/Corbis 3 CL © Yann Arthus-Bertrand/Corbis 3 CR © Comstock/Corbis 4 BL © Tom Brakefield/Corbis 5 CL © filonmar/iStockphoto 5 CL © Jean-François Héroux/iStockphoto 5 CR © Anthony Berenyi/Shutterstock 5 CR © Fedor Selivanov/Shutterstock 5 BL © Roger Ressmeyer/Corbis 6 BR © Stock Connection Blue/Alamy 12 CL © AP Photo/Shizuo Kambayashi/La Presse Canadienne 15 BL © Getty Images 15 BR © Time & Life Pictures/Getty Images 16 CL © Christopher Edwin Nuzzaco/Shutterstock 23 BC © Bettmann/Corbis 25 CL © Kingston Whig-Standard - Michael Lea/La Presse Canadienne 26 BL © mehmetsait/Shutterstock 26 BC © Science Photo Library/Alamy 26 BR © Wang Jiaowen/Color China Photos/ZUMA/KEYSTONE Press 27 BR © Adrian Bradshaw/epa/Corbis 34 TR © Thomas Sztanek/Shutterstock 34 CR © Milan Keser/Shutterstock 35 BR © Medical RF.com/Science Photo Library/Publiphoto 37 TL © Losevsky Pavel/Shutterstock 37 TR © James Steidl/Shutterstock 38 BL © Bettmann/Corbis 42 CL © Maurizio Gambarini/dpa/Corbis 43 TR © Rosenfeld Images Ltd/SPL/Publiphoto 43 BR © mrfotos/Shutterstock 44 BL © PhotoSpin, Inc/Alamy 45 BR © Nikita Tiunov/Shutterstock 47 BC © Debra James/Shutterstock 48 CR © Owaki - Kulla/Corbis 48 BR © AgStock Images/Corbis 49 M © Gareth Byrne/Alamy 51 BG © Gustavo Miguel Machado da Caridade Fernandes/Shutterstock 51 BC © Natalie Fobes/Corbis 58 TR © Terri Francis/Shutterstock 58 CR © ArtmannWitte/Shutterstock 59 BC © Roger Ressmeyer/Corbis 60 BL © Megapress.ca/Philiptchenko 60 BR © PictureNet/Corbis 61 BR © Monkey Business Images/Shutterstock 62 TL © Photo courtesy of INFORMS 62 BL © Hulton-Deutsch Collection/Corbis 62 BR © Corbis 63 BL © Corbis 64 TL © Jonathan Hayward/La Presse Canadienne 64 BL © Patrick Robert/Sygma/Corbis 64 BR © Charles Caratini/Sygma/Corbis 65 TR © Thomas Hartwell/Corbis 68 CL © Canadian Museum of Civilization/Corbis 71 CR © Kiselev Andrey Valerevich/Shutterstock 73 TR © Christian Darkin/SPL/Publiphoto 74 TR © Fotocrisis/Shutterstock 75 BR © Wolfgang Kaehler/Corbis 76 CR © ricardo azoury/iStockphoto 77 BR © GARY I ROTHSTEIN/epa/Corbis

Vision 2

79 TL © Alexander Kolomietz/Shutterstock 79 TR © Paul A. Souders/Corbis 79 CL © Claudio Arnese/iStockphoto 79 CR © Rui Vale de Sousa/Shutterstock 80 BR © Mimmo Jodice/Corbis 81 BC © Simfo/iStockphoto 87 CR © Kenneth William Caleno/Shutterstock 87 BL © Dorling Kindersley/Getty 87 BC © Kenneth Libbrecht/Science Photo Library/Publiphoto 87 BR © Martin Kubát/Shutterstock 89 BL © Joshua Shrader/Shutterstock 90 BR © ARCTIC IMAGES/Alamy 91 M © M.C. Escher's Eight Heads 2009 The M.C. Escher Company-Holland. All rights reserved 92 M © M.C. Escher's Symmetry Drawing E45 2009 The M.C. Escher Company-Holland. All rights reserved 93 M © M.C. Escher's Symmetry Drawing E91 2009 The M.C. Escher Company-Holland. All rights reserved 103 TR © CHINA PHOTOS/Reuters/Corbis 104 BL © Alinari Archives/Corbis 105 CL © Mark De Fraeye/Science Photo Library/Publiphoto 105 BL © Skyscan/Science Photo Library/Publiphoto 112 TL © Andrew F. Kazmierski/Shutterstock 112 TR © Andrew F. Kazmierski/Shutterstock 113 BR © Gerrit/Shutterstock 114 BL © jolka/Shutterstock 115 BL © Eremin Sergey/Shutterstock 115 BR © Ric Ergenbright/Corbis 116 TR © Tina Rencelj/Shutterstock 117 B © Megapress.ca 122 BL © Rob Byron/Shutterstock 122 BR © mtsyri/Shutterstock 123 BR © Rob Wilson/Shutterstock 134 CR © Linda & Colin McKie/iStockphoto 134 BL © Bettmann/Corbis 134 BR © JackF/Shutterstock 135 TR © plastique/Shutterstock 136 TL © Megapress.ca 136 CR © Sebastian Kaulitzki/Shutterstock 137 CL © STILLFX/Shutterstock 138 TL © Royalty-free photo 138 BL © bleex/iStockphoto 140 TL © André Klaassen/Shutterstock 141 TR © Volker Steger/Science Photo Library/Publiphoto 141 CR © Lyle Stafford/Reuters/Corbis 149 CL © kolvenbach/Alamy 149 CR © Vladone/iStockphoto 149 BR © Stephen Finn/Alamy 150 TR © Ruth Black/Shutterstock 151 BL © Iourii Tcheka/Shutterstock 152 TR © Alistair Cotton/Shutterstock

LES

156 CR © Khlobystov Alexey/Shutterstock 156 BL © ELEN/Shutterstock 156 BR © Image Source/Corbis 157 TR © Denis Vrublevski/Shutterstock 158 CR © Jaimie Duplass/Shutterstock 158 BG © Kheng Guan Toh/Shutterstock 160 TR © Josef Bosak/Shutterstock 160 BL © Blackout Concepts/Alamy 160 BR © Baloncici/Shutterstock 161 TR © Baloncici/Shutterstock 161 BC © Hintau Aliaksei/Shutterstock 162 TR © twobluedogs/Shutterstock 162 CL © Galyna Andrushko/Shutterstock 163 TR © Vladimir Mucibabic/Shutterstock 163 CL © Servifoto/iStockphoto 163 CR © NatashaBo/Shutterstock